Individualized Teaching in Elementary Schools

Dona Kofod Stahl

Patricia Murphy Anzalone

Individualized Teaching
in Elementary Schools

Parker Publishing Company, Inc.   West Nyack, N.Y

to

OUR CHILDREN

each one uniquely individual

Acknowledgments

We are most grateful to those who have influenced our thinking and guided us in our efforts toward individualizing instruction and to those who have inspired, spurred, and assisted us in the preparation of this book:

—To H. Edward Litteer, Principal of the Floyd Winslow School, who believes in the self-actualization of his staff and continuous progress for each child and who started us off on the road to professional introspection.

—To Dr. Elizabeth Z. Howard for her devotion to the uniqueness of the individual and for her encouragement to explore and develop our commitments.

—To Miss Elizabeth Noon, who felt we had something to say and encouraged us to say it.

—To Dr. Donald D. Durrell and his associates at Boston University from whom stem many of the ideas and practices in pupil-team learning discussed in this book.

—To the elementary curriculum staff at Wellesley, Massachusetts, who first introduced us to pupil-team techniques.

—To Dr. Marjorie Seddon Johnson, who stimulated our thinking about better questioning techniques.

—To Dr. Jerome P. Lysaught, who helped us explore the quality of objectives we set for a teaching-learning environment.

—To the faculty and staff of the Winslow School in Rush-Henrietta, who share with us their ideas, time, and effort as we search for better ways of meeting the needs of each child.

—To Mrs. Hattie L. Kofod who generously assisted in proofreading and to Mrs. Joyce L. Kofod and Mrs. Hazel L. Boyd who typed the manuscript.

—And above all to our families whose love and understanding provided the supporting environment necessary for this endeavor.

Some of the material in this book originally appeared in an article by the authors in the May 1967 issue of *The Instructor*, The Instructor Publications, Inc.

D.K.S.
P.M.A.

You Can Do
Something About
Individualizing Instruction

Much has been said among educators about individual differences and the resulting need for individualized teaching in the schools. The major purpose of this book is to provide some specific, concrete suggestions for putting theory about individualizing instruction into realistic, workable, effective practice. It includes many ideas for modifying standard classroom procedures which teachers may wish to adopt or adapt to their own situations. These are suggestions which can be incorporated into any type of school—urban, rural, suburban, or inner-city—without requiring changes in organizational patterns.

The book is organized into four parts, each focusing upon individualization of instruction from a different viewpoint. The first part considers the rationale for individualizing instruction. It looks at some assumptions we make about the child as a learner and about the educator's responsibility to the uniqueness of the child. It discusses some implications of individualizing instruction in terms of the new role of the teacher. The second part is devoted to considering strategies for individualization. These are educational methods which can be utilized in this approach to teaching. Techniques which can be used within the framework of the strategies are discussed in the third part. Suggestions and examples are drawn from many subject areas and grade levels. The final section of the book focuses upon various aspects of providing and preparing instructional materials to be used in a program of differentiated instruction.

Individualized instruction is not a clearly defined point at which we arrive in teaching as much as it is a target at which we aim and toward which we progress. This book has been designed to provide a way to share with teachers the ideas, experiences, and ambitions of the authors in their attempts at individualizing instruction. It is essentially an *idea* book rather than an *answer* book. We invite you to browse in it, think about it, and use it in whatever way will best help you in planning your own program of differentiated instruction. It is hoped that some of the suggestions and ideas contained in the book will provide a jumping-off place for the further consideration and subsequent action of those involved in education. Accept parts of it when you can; reject parts of it as we know you must; modify parts of it to make them fit you and your needs. Come back to it from time to time as your thinking and efforts move you along toward individualizing instruction.

D.K.S.

P.M A.

Contents

11

10. Guided Listening Activities *(Continued)*

Mathematics ● Directing Concrete Experiences ● Providing Opportunities for Drill and Practice ● Following Directions

STRUCTURING LISTENING ACTIVITIES FOR INDEPENDENT LEARNING   140
Check Lists ● Listening Guides

MANIPULATIVES AT THE PREREADING LEVEL   145
Developing Readiness Skills with Beads ● Level 1 ● Level II ● Level III ● Construction Toys ● Level 1 ● Level II ● Level III ● A Multimedia Approach to Manipulatives ● Blocks as Media for Developing Spatial Perceptions

TOYS AND GAMES BEYOND THE PRIMARY LEVEL   149
Selecting Games for the Classroom

Habits and Attitudes Conducive to Self-Directed Learning ● Motivation ● Errors ● Consideration for Others

INSTEAD OF SEATWORK   162
Science Corner ● Math Table ● Prehistoric Animal Race ● Set Formation ● Other Centers of Interest

PUPIL-TAUGHT LESSONS   168
Map of the World ● Three-Dimensional Map of the Southwest ● Drawing of Land Forms ● Animal Drawings ● Diorama of Cactus Plants ● Transparencies of Cactus Plants ● Diorama of Irrigation System ● Graph of Agricultural Yields

A SUGGESTION BOX   172
Science Suggestions

A Precautionary Reminder

HOMEWORK FOR EACH CHILD   178
Differentiating with a Single Textbook ● Something for the Classroom ● Making Math Materials ● Art Lending Library

ONE

The Effective Teacher and Individualized Instruction

The time is 1:20. The planbook calls for social studies

"Boys and girls, please open your social studies books to page 205." *I wonder if I should close the blinds so Jimmy and Steve can't stare out the window as they so often do?*

"Yesterday, you will remember, we talked about the Louisiana Purchase." *I hope Tom will pay attention today. He often tells me such interesting things about pioneers and explorers. I wonder why he is so bored with the Westward Movement unit?*

"Today we are going to read about two men who explored the Louisiana Territory." *Don't look so worried, Mary Jo. It won't be your turn to read aloud today. What makes you afraid of everything?*

"On page 205, find the section entitled, 'Lewis and Clark Explore the Louisiana Territory.' " *But what am I going to do about Sam? His turn to read will come today and I know he can't manage this book. Will he feel left out if I just skip over him or would it be worse to let him struggle through a paragraph?*

"Put away the drawing paper, Suzanne, and try to concentrate on social studies." *What is there about that girl! No matter what the rest of the class is doing it seems she just wants to sit and draw pictures.*

"No, Pat, we are not going to be writing answers to questions

17

today." *I know that will make you happy. We really must do something about your writing!*

"Terry, would you please read the first column?" *Thank goodness for Terry! She can read anything well. . . . I'd better keep an eye on Lois. She is apt to be playing with something inside her desk instead of keeping her place in the book. . . . And there's Ralph getting ready to throw a piece of paper at Billy. . . . Oh dear! There must be another way to teach social studies—something that will be right for all of them.*

Another way to teach social studies? Yes, of course, there are many other ways. Several possibilities come almost immediately to mind—lectures, movies, reports, class discussions, worksheets, dioramas or other projects. But a way that will be right for all of the children? What way will be right for the child who struggles with second-grade reading materials and yet meet the needs of a child who comprehends junior high texts? Will the child who is already something of an expert on a topic benefit from a program designed for one who has no familiarity at all with the topic? Look around you at the children in any classroom. Is there one who talks much of the time and another who rarely speaks even when you want him to? Can you find one who has the self-confidence to tackle anything and another who has to be assured that every step he takes is all right? Perhaps you recognize a child who would be content to read all day and see another who cannot sit still for five minutes. There may be one highly motivated child and another who "couldn't care less." What single way to teach will be right for all of these?

The dilemma with which our hypothetical teacher is faced in teaching her social studies lesson is basically the same problem confronting teachers all across the country. How do we plan an instructional program which will accommodate the differences we find among the students in our classrooms? As educators, we must feel an obligation to provide the best possible learning opportunities for each child.

THE CHILD AND LEARNING

Some of the most vital learnings that take place in our schools never appear as objectives in the teacher's plan book. They are the things a child is learning to think about himself. Such learnings cannot be classified as part of a reading or a math lesson, yet they take place during these times; they take place anywhere and anytime during the day. The things a child learns to think about himself may sometimes be desirable and at other times be quite undesirable, but they are always vital. The way a child feels about himself will affect everything he does in school or out of it. It will set the pattern for his behavior throughout life. Every day, the experiences he has in school will add something to his self-picture. Are we helping him build success, interest, and vitality or are we teaching him frustration, boredom, and defeat?

Negative learnings increase as schools become more concerned with average pupil behavior and use these averages as a yardstick of expectancy to evaluate individuals. The *average* child might learn to read at six but a perfectly *normal* individual might not develop sufficient skills for initial reading instruction until eight. The average ten-year-old might be able to learn 20 new spelling words each week, but some normal ten-year-olds might consistently master 30 words a week and others only six. Perhaps a more realistic yardstick would be one which *expects* children to be different and which *encourages* the development of uniqueness.

We must look at each child as a truly important individual—as a person worth our interest and effort. We must realize that each child is capable of learning something. There is nothing which helps a child feel good about himself more than a sense of accomplishment. Provide the child with many opportunities to achieve success and you will provide him with many opportunities to experience pride and self-satisfaction. This can be done only if he is given tasks which it is possible for him to do. It means the teacher will be placed in a position where it is essential to differentiate instruction in order to find just the right tasks and experiences for each child. To ask all children at a given age or in a given grade to learn the same way or to do the same work in spelling, English, arithmetic, or any other subject is as unrealistic as asking them all to wear the same size clothing.

As a child grows in his feeling of self-confidence, it is possible for him to develop a high degree of independence and self-direction. One of our major goals should be to have all children become more actively involved in the constructive direction of their own activities. The child who does develop this kind of independence is, at the same time, developing a better picture of himself and his worth as an individual.

In planning to provide for each child, careful consideration should be given to the sequential development of skills and concepts. We cannot expect a child to solve complicated problems involving multiple variables until he has mastered the ability to handle simpler kinds of problems. It is important to pace the sequence of experiences in developing skills and concepts so as to provide sufficient opportunity for each child to master each phase of the program. It is unfortunately easy for teachers to assume that because a few children give the desired response and appear to have mastered the desired skill, all the children are ready to go on by virtue of having heard a correct response. Now is the time to remember that active, not passive, participation is necessary for mastery of any skill. Each child must become actively involved in the development and application of those skills and concepts which are appropriate for him.

THE TEACHER

These statements about children and learning have direct implications for the classroom teacher. They imply basically that he must be dedicated to the goal of individualization of instruction. Admittedly this is an ideal, but it is one toward which we can actively work. Planning, persevering and hard work are essential. You will also find it important to maintain open lines of two-way communication between yourself and your principal, your pupils, and their parents. A sincere, highly motivated commitment to providing the best possible learning opportunities for each child is your strongest asset. This dedication to individualization carries with it a willingness to engage in some rather extensive introspection and retrospection, to approach new ideas with an open mind, and to perceive the teacher as filling a new and increasingly complex role.

At one time the teacher's responsibility was seen largely as transmitting information—teaching lessons and covering material. It was up to each pupil to learn the lessons and material. If a child didn't learn, it was because he was lazy, had poor work habits, just didn't care, or had various kinds of problems stemming from home. This concept has given way to the idea that the teacher's responsibility doesn't end until the child *has* learned. Learning has taken place when the desired change in behavior has occurred. The day is rapidly disappearing when a teacher will stand before a class of thirty students and present a lesson on "how to do long division" or "the causes of the American Revolution." The new role of the teacher is emerging as a complex of roles. He must be at once a diagnostician, a materials specialist, and a learning consultant.

A Diagnostician. Today's teacher is involved in appraising the readiness a learner brings to a task. There are elements of readiness in each new task a child undertakes. We cannot be satisfied with knowing when he is ready to *start* reading or *start* arithmetic. We must try to determine readiness for each step he takes as he continues reading, arithmetic, or any other subject. A consideration of readiness includes an investigation of prior learnings and any misconceptions a child might bring to a new learning situation. The child who has traveled widely in many states might not need the same experiences in a study of United States geography as does a child who thinks New Mexico is another country and Los Angeles is a state somewhere near California.

Diagnosis means learning all you can about each child. Know his instructional level in reading, but also know the reading level at which he can work independently without frustration. Assess the rate at which a child works, the things which interest him, his willingness to tackle a new task and to stay with it. Determine the child's ability to profit from self-evaluation, his tolerance of failure, his own appraisal of himself as a learner and as a person.

Having learned as much as possible about each child, you can use this information as the basis for planning his instructional program. This may mean establishing different goals for some children than for others and will probably require mapping out different learning routes for some children to follow in working toward their goals. Depth of knowledge about each child points up the need for a variety of ways to work with the pupils. The differentiating of pupil goals, learning routes, and instructional methods implies a corresponding approach to pupil evaluation.

Your goal in planning for instruction is not that of finding a direction in which to point the whole class. You must find a variety of directions in which to point a variety of individuals or small groups of pupils. Diagnosis should provide you with the raw materials from which to build the framework for a program of individualized instruction.

A Materials Specialist. Education is no longer a one-way street. Today there are many ways and media for making learning more effective and, at the same time, more stimulating for both pupil and teacher. In order to provide different learning routes for children, we must be familiar with a variety of instructional materials and equipment. This means knowing the readability level of material and the difficulty of the tasks involved. An understanding of the purpose of the material and how well it meets its objectives is necessary before we can hope to use it wisely. The content covered in a given instructional material may be an important consideration. The teacher is faced with the need to analyze the various materials available to him in terms of the learning needs which exist in his classroom and select those which seem most appropriate for specific children.

When suitable instructional materials are not available for certain pupils or for some special study, it may be necessary for the teacher to prepare his own. This is not a difficult task, especially if several teachers who will use the material share the work and their ideas. Often you will find that maintaining a file of teacher-made materials will serve some of your needs another year as well.

A Learning Consultant. In addition to being a diagnostician and materials specialist, the effective teacher serves as a learning consultant to his students. This implies providing assistance and guidance in learning rather than using a force-feeding approach. You will find it necessary to work with the entire class less frequently. The introduction of new skills and concepts may be handled with smaller groups. There will be many opportunities to arrange for children to work together, assisting and learning from each other.

In problem-solving situations, the teacher assists the student in the development of his ability to focus on and delineate a problem. You find that as a consultant you listen more and talk less. You give a pupil guidance as he analyzes alternative solutions to his problem and seeks to select his own most satisfactory answer. If we wish our pupils to approach learning with critical, yet open-minded attitudes, we must serve as models for this type of behavior. While demanding high standards of academic work, we should retain a willingness to accept divergent thinking and styles of learning. This is the type of thinking which will lead to future discoveries, inventions, and innovations in our world. To develop the unique individuals which society needs, we must attempt not to extrude education through the same mold for all youngsters.

Teaching which is at once diagnostic and individualized can enable children to progress along a continuum of small and successful steps. Periodic evaluation by the teacher can measure mastery of each level as the child progresses. When the child desires the goal, has been involved in evaluating his own learning, realizes the value of his achievements, and knows what he must yet attain, we can expect him to realize much of the potential which is uniquely his own.

SUMMARY

Teachers continually search for better, more effective ways of helping children learn. The whole-class approach to instruction is found to be inadequate for meeting individual differences and needs in the classroom. No single method can be considered *the best* method just as no method can be categorically labeled inappropriate. Fortunately we can draw from numerous and varied instructional strategies, techniques, and activities, each of which can be effectively utilized for some children in some situations some of the time. The challenge of individualizing instruction is that of finding a better "fit" for each child when planning an instructional program. Your role as teacher becomes increasingly complex. *You* must find the best fit for each child you work with. This is not easy.

Our commitment to individualized instruction is based on the following hypotheses about children and learning. The activities, suggestions, and experiences contained in the following chapters have been built upon them.

1. There are many patterns of learning and no one teaching method meets the varied needs of all children. It is vitally important to provide alternatives in the educational program.
2. The teacher cannot tell a child how to think, but must provide him with the freedom, the encouragement, and the opportunity to do so.
3. Learning is an active, not a passive, process and must involve participation in a task rather than mere absorption of information. As a result of learning there should be a change in pupil behavior or no learning has taken place.
4. Children are consistent in their need for success experiences, but vary greatly in their levels and rates of achievement.
5. Discovering and developing uniqueness in individuals is a major goal not to be thwarted by ignoring or minimizing differences.
6. Children bring to each new experience varying amounts of information and misinformation, which may clarify or distort concept formation.
7. Setting goals and evaluating progress are the privilege and the responsibility of the child, and are essential to long-term learning. Teachers must not let a marking system distort evaluation.
8. The unstructured and inductive experiences which occur in a child's life are often the most profound and influential activities of childhood.
9. Children learn from each other, through observation, imitation, and cooperative consideration of a mutually challenging task.
10. Learning is both positive and negative. When the activity does not fit the child's unique personal need, negative learning is certain to occur.
11. It is more important for children to appreciate and practice self-control than to be controlled by an adult authority figure.
12. Intrinsic motivation makes children capable of meaningful self-selection and self-correction of appropriate learning activities.

TWO

The Challenge
of the Change

Transposing instructional theory into instructional practice is an open-ended task which often appears impossible to achieve. Certainly accepting the goal of individualizing instruction presents the teacher with a challenge which must be approached with both patience and creativity. Teachers attempting to make this transition tend to ask certain common questions which are generally concerned with pinpointing what is meant by individualized instruction, what changes will be involved, and what problems will be encountered in this approach. Perhaps you have posed some of these questions.

Does Individualized Instruction Mean Teaching on a One-to-One Basis All Day?

If your concept of individualized instruction is a continual series of paired situations, teacher and student, reason and experience will tell you that this kind of individualization is impossible. A strictly tutorial relationship is not only impossible but also not truly desirable if we value the social learnings and skills which are acquired only by working within groups. Occasionally it will be necessary to work with one child, but you can use many other strategies to differentiate instruction.

Are the Terms Differentiate and Individualize Synonymous?

To truly individualize instruction we would probably have to provide every child with a unique set of learning experiences. We might also find it necessary to provide each student with a unique set of teachers—teachers who are expert in recognizing and developing the many facets of that learner's potential. Differentiating instruction is a realistic step toward the ideal of individualized instruction. You differentiate when you recognize and accept the different learning needs within the class and modify your methods to meet some of those needs.

CHANGES

A major modification in instructional strategies such as the move toward individualized instruction is accompanied by certain changes. Changes should be expected in the physical and psychological environment of the classroom. The ways in which teacher and pupils utilize time and materials and the kinds of activities they undertake will differ from those of a whole-class approach. The results of such a program will reflect the change in emphasis from grade level expectations and competition to individual expectations based upon realistic goals for each pupil. The teacher preparing to make this modification in his instructional program will do well to be aware of some of the changes which will be involved.

What External Changes Can a Teacher Expect as He Moves to Differentiated Instruction?

Your classroom will become the setting for an experience in cooperative group living. You will be encouraging children to learn in varied ways, often working cooperatively. As a result, children will become less competitive. Your room environment will be created in terms of personal and group efficiency rather than the traditional standards of quietness. There will often be a much higher level of noise. Pupil activity will not revolve around your personality although you remain the most influential person there. You will guide the pupils in developing their own value systems as you encourage them to set standards for classroom behavior. The children will gradually assume some of the responsibility for setting goals and instructional objectives, first as a group and later as individuals.

Time will be utilized differently. The schedule will be more flexible, with larger blocks of time to allow children to become more involved with learning and to pursue their interests in depth. Some children will spend more time on one subject than another. It will become impossible for you to meet with every child in every subject every day. Subgroups will form or be formed in all subjects to investigate different aspects of a concept or to work at different applications of a skill.

You will employ a multisensory approach to learning with far more varied materials designed to stimulate visual, auditory, and tactile responses. Many children will use manipulative devices and games as primary learning materials rather than as supplemental activities. Children will be encouraged to create ways to communicate what they have been learning. Ongoing projects of varying types and duration will often replace whole-class tests as a measure of individual progress and understanding. Because of this variety of activity, your room—though efficiently organized for the needs of the children—may appear disorderly by some adult standards.

What Change in My Teaching Style Will Be Most Evident?

Discussions involving inquiry or discovery will replace much of the lecture approach. Such methods promote the formulation and testing of ideas and hypotheses. You will guide children to find answers rather than tell them answers. A child will be en couraged to "try it and see for yourself" in science more often than he will be asked to watch a teacher demonstrate an experiment for the whole class, giving explanations of *why* and *how* at each step of the lesson. Questioning takes on a new importance. Questions will be used for diagnosis and for stimulating children's thinking more frequently than for recitation or testing. A social studies lesson, for example, may focus on having children pose questions for subsequent study rather than on having children respond to questions posed by the teacher.

As you work for individually tailored programs, the textbook will no longer determine classroom procedure. Use will be found for a variety of textbooks, trade books, and other commercial materials, but few, if any, grade level sets with a copy for every child will be found appropriate. You will discover many ways to supply the need for variety and flexibility in instructional materials.

An inexpensive way to provide a wide variety of multilevel reading material in several areas was found by one resourceful upper primary teacher. After collecting many copies of books which had been discarded, publishers' samples and assorted children's magazines, she tore out portions of each and assembled each story or article into a booklet. Colored oaktag was used for covers—green for science articles, red for fiction, blue for social studies, etc. Each booklet had an additional coding system. A colored star was used to indicate the specific area or subtopic which was covered in the selection. For example, on the green science booklets, red stars tagged articles about space. This coding system simplified the selection and returning of booklets by the children. Much of the actual construction of the booklets was done by the children after the coding classifications had been determined.

Homework, in the sense of everyone reading pages 45–52 in the social studies book, will be replaced by something more in keeping with individualized programs. Less time will need to be spent in marking papers or hearing children perform. You can devote more time to pupil conferences involving two-way communication. Out-of-class time will be used to gain background in various subjects and in preparing work materials tailored to children's individual needs.

You will constantly be alert to better means of evaluating. Children will take an active part in their own evaluation and will come to realize that grading is only one phase of evaluation. Tests will be given to children as they are ready to be tested and, with the exception of standardized tests, rarely to the whole group at the same time.

What New Satisfactions Might Offset the Obvious Expenditure of Time and Effort?

You will be less likely to have children who are failing in their work because each learning sequence will be designed to permit each child to succeed at an appropriate level.

Children will view themselves and others more realistically. As you discover and capitalize on individual strengths, the children in your class will adopt a positive way of regarding other children. You will know your children better. They will become increasingly different rather than more alike as time goes along. As their special talents and interests become evident and are cultivated, you will find all children more interesting and fun to work with.

Your relationship with parents will be strengthened. Misunderstandings happen less frequently when you can communicate your knowledge of and plans for a given child. Parents recognize and appreciate the teacher who can discuss the specific goals and achievements of their child and not merely talk about the class or children in general. The success that children are having will be reflected in the positive attitudes of the parents.

Will Children Learn as Much as They Do in the Traditional Classroom?

Some will "learn" less, some far more if we consider only the content area of the curriculum. Traditional, whole-class teaching might guarantee that each child will be exposed to a given body of information, but it has never succeeded in guaranteeing equal understanding by all children. The habit of non-participation and disinterest will be replaced by a willingness to attempt a variety of tasks. Positive learnings which lie outside the realm of content will be increased for all. Children will learn to utilize many sources to find answers. Leadership skills will be developed in children who formerly were considered followers. Children who were convinced of their own inferiority will learn that they are capable and worthwhile students who can achieve success in school.

PROBLEMS

Being alert to potential problems often makes it possible to take steps which will avoid or minimize them. Some things which may at first appear to be problems merely represent changes which, after more careful analysis, are found to be desirable. The attitude with which you approach the change may easily turn a potential problem into a challenging adventure. You may find that some of the problems which you had anticipated never actually materialize. Those problems which do confront you can be handled more smoothly and quickly if you expect them and have done whatever you can to prepare for them.

Are There Any Real Pitfalls to Be Alert to?

Trying to proceed too rapidly will soon leave you discouraged. As you strive to give less direction and to help children become objective about their work, you may at times become frustrated. You will soon realize that a poor teacher who can keep the children quiet is less likely to encounter difficulty than a creative teacher who has not ironed out all the kinks of a new process.

There are a few suggestions which might help you retain your sense of equilibrium during the getting started period. Expect more noise and seeming confusion than you are used to, but notice that it is probably working noise made by many children actively engaged in a learning experience. The apparent confusion may mean merely that you have not yet become accustomed to greater and more varied activity. Thoughtful organization of the classroom may alleviate some unnecessary moving about.

Expect some days to be better than others, some programs to work more smoothly than others, and some children to operate more independently than others. Above all, don't expect to perform miracles overnight. Such an attitude could result in early discouragement and lead you into the temptation of giving it all up. If you do feel this way, give it up for a week or two and then start it again gradually.

Won't Instructional Materials Be a Problem?

There are many types of materials currently available and publishers will continue to produce many kinds which are suitable for differentiated instruction. Programmed materials (the kind usually associated with teaching machines) can be found in all subjects and at all levels. Self-instructional kit-type materials designed primarily to meet differences in level and rate are available in a variety of skill development packages at all levels. Textbooks, of course, can be provided from several series, and at several grade levels. There are also trade books and reference materials at many readability levels. Specific instructional materials discussed throughout the book are listed in the Appendix.

The whole area of audio-visual equipment and materials offers a wide range of possibilities. Films, slides, filmstrips, single concept film loops, records, tapes, and overhead transparencies are available in most schools. There is nothing new about the idea of using these materials, but we need to take a new look at *how* we use them. Is it necessary to show a film to the whole class? Do we need to use all of the frames on a filmstrip? Multimedia packages which combine visual and audio materials are on the market. Similar packages can be improvised by combining many of the materials you may have on hand.

We tend to overlook other readily available material simply because it is not labelled *educational material*. Pictures, games and toys, common household items, a handful of gravel, a bunch of safety pins—these can all become educational when you are alert to and consciously searching for more effective and efficient ways of providing for the learning need of each child. The abundance, variety, and sources of instructional materials are limited more by lack of imagination and ingenuity than by a tight budget.

Will It Be Difficult to Maintain Classroom Control and Discipline?

Boredom, disinterest, and frustration are the authors of most tales of classroom mismanagement. Disinterest with the teacher's proposed activity yields minimal performance in many students and a complete refusal to perform in others. Work which is too difficult for a child will frustrate that child. He will not learn what the teacher intended him to learn, but he will learn the futility of trying and this will also be expressed in undesirable pupil behavior. Once the classroom environment serves the varying needs of individual learners, the problems of classroom control will be minimized.

Our real concern is to develop self-controlled and independent learners. The authors have experienced and witnessed many occasions where entire classes of children—"discipline problems" as well as "good students," first graders as well as older children—were able to carry on with their individualized learning programs completely without adult assistance or control for periods ranging from an hour to half a day.   owever, we must not expect a room of 30 children to work any more quietly than a room of 30 adults would. Some conversation and moving about is necessary—more of it than with teacher-centered activities. You should even expect the children to take occasional breaks from their work. A conversation among several children which does not re late to school work can give them a welcome and relaxing change during their working day, just as an exchange of pleasantries between teachers can temper the pace of the teaching day.

These have been typical of the questions asked by teachers embarking on programs of differentiated instruction. The comments following each have been just that. Comments. Perhaps there have been the beginnings of some answers. If you are looking for *the* answer to individualizing instruction, you won't find it in this book. Here you will find suggestions, ideas, and experiences that have worked for *some* teachers. Each teacher must find many ways to approach individualization. You will reject many of the suggestions that follow. A few of them you may be able to use just as they are described. Most of them you will need to modify or adapt to your own style and purposes. Teachers, too, have individual differences.

THREE

Grouping Patterns for Differentiated Instruction

Grouping children within a class is essential if you are going to act upon your commitment to individualize instruction. The three basic grouping patterns—whole class, small group, and individual instruction—are fundamental and familiar to all teachers. Differentiated instruction demands that each be used at some time and for some children.

The purpose of any learning sequence will frequently be the most important single factor in determining the organizational grouping patterns which a teacher establishes. The teacher must first determine whether a given learning will be effectively enhanced for a given child and whether time will be utilized efficiently before deciding which grouping pattern to use. Frequently a combination of grouping patterns will be the most effective and efficient way to serve the needs of individual learners. The discussion which follows is designed to help you to design a flexible organizational grouping pattern.

WORKING WITH THE WHOLE CLASS

Individualized instruction does not negate the appropriateness of whole-class instruction. Much of what we need to know

33

about the unique characteristics of a given child can be learned by observing the way he acts and reacts within a large group. Lessons which consist of a lecture by the teacher or which are merely round robin recitations are not suitable for this type of observation. It is possible though to learn much about children when you ask open-ended questions—questions which have many possible answers. Should pet owners be asked to keep their animals penned up or on a leash? What characteristics do great men share? Would you classify Adolph Hitler as a great man?

Each open-ended question should be followed by a second question which asks the learner to give reasons for answering in a particular way. You will get the most mileage out of questions of this type when you are freely accepting of children's answers. It is important that you reserve value judgments. When a child's response seems to be morbid or an attempt at humor, additional questions can be asked to clarify the child's thinking. It takes practice and patience to develop the ability to direct whole-class discussions which do not cut off children's thinking. Too frequently we as teachers have predetermined the *right* answers, and are so eager to have children vocalize *our* answers that we fail to develop *theirs*.

Learning About Attitudes and Interests

Some questions can be asked which allow every child to give a unique yet correct answer. The answers to these questions furnish teachers with important information about the attitudes and interests of individual children. The following might be asked of every child in the group.

1. What do you like to do on a rainy day?
2. What is your favorite toy? Why did you choose it as your favorite?
3. If someone gave you a dollar what would you buy with it?
4. How many brothers and sisters do you have and what are their names and ages?
5. If you could relive any day, which one would it be? What kind of a day was it?
6. If you were the principal of our school what four changes would you make?

7. If you could be someone else, who would it be? Why did you answer this way?
8. What would you have for dinner tonight if you could have anything you wanted?
9. Why do children have to go to school?
10. What jobs do you do at home?

Recording the answers to questions like these poses a different problem for early primary children who have not learned to read and write. These children can record their answers by drawing or by cutting illustrations from magazines, while the teacher circulates among the group, observing and questioning.

Establishing Routines

When the nature of a given activity requires that strict standards be observed by all, whole-class instruction is often the most efficient way to train children. The forms which you require for headings, the way chairs are to be carried, conduct during a fire drill and other no-decision behaviors you expect of all children are essentially whole-class training activities. If your class is to be self-directing it is important that each of these standards be understood and followed by all.

A classroom environment which allows children to choose from a variety of activities will be successful to the degree that children are capable of assuming the responsibility for the care of materials and equipment. Whole class instruction in obtaining and storing materials is essential before children can be expected to assume this responsibility.

Art projects such as dioramas, murals and models are favorites of many children, but they can become nightmares when undertaken without advance consideration of potential problems. Each child needs to know exactly how to open a jar of paint, carry scissors, clean up a spill, wash and store brushes. He must know where to store incomplete projects, wet paintings, and pieces of something that he didn't get glued on yet.

The possibility of confusion is of concern to many teachers contemplating a major shift toward individualization. This confusion can be avoided by analyzing the nature of the responsibilities children can and should assume. Training is the next logical step. Training is a hard and rather unprofessional word for educators, but certain routines are things we do not allow children to make decisions about for themselves. The child may choose to paint, but he may not choose to avoid the responsibility painting entails.

Children who are being introduced to new materials will profit from whole-class instruction in how to use them, how to keep records, and how to evaluate their work realistically. You will probably want children to follow a set standard for marking incorrect answers on their own papers. Children frequently find that although their answer is different from the key, it is still correct. Standard ways to disagree with an answer key must be established.

One or two whole-group lessons should be devoted to the procedure for analyzing errors. The overhead projector is an excellent device for this type of whole group lesson. Samples of student work can be reproduced (deleting the students' names) and projected for the entire class to analyze. Was the question misunderstood? Did the student follow directions? Is this another slant toward the problem and equally or partially correct?

Frequently we focus on what a child does not know and attach great importance to every error children make. Wrong is simply *all* wrong and is rarely analyzed. The effective teacher must develop each child's ability to accept an incorrect answer as an opportunity to learn. Why an answer is wrong is far more important than the simple fact that it is wrong.

WORKING WITH SMALL GROUPS

Working with subgroups of six to twelve in reading is a common practice. Children are usually clustered on the basis of some degree of alikeness or readiness for instruction. A few children needing extra work in identifying initial consonant sounds may comprise one group while several other children who are ready to move on to a more advanced skill form another group. While small-group instruction is not the only way to meet individual needs, extending this practice to subjects other than reading is certainly one good way to work toward individualized teaching.

Math is a good place to begin forming subgroups because diagnosis and evaluation are less subjective. When you have a group of children who are ready for a new skill or concept, plan to work closely with them for several days while introducing the new work. As soon as you are confident that each child understands how to proceed with independent practice materials, the group can meet without you. You will continue to meet with members of the group from time to time to evaluate progress, give assistance in difficult areas and present new concepts and new materials. Having started one group on a program of independent activities, you are freed to work with the remainder of the class, eventually establishing other subgroups for specialized instruction and regrouping when necessary.

One generalization which should serve as a guide in establishing independent groups is to begin with groups of children who are most apt to succeed. As teachers we are constantly searching for time to help the slower child. By developing independence first in the more able students, you will find that you have more time and energy to help all children.

WORKING WITH INDIVIDUALS

As children develop independent work habits you will find yourself assuming a classroom consultant role more frequently. One-to-one instruction may often be the most efficient and effective way to work with children in the development of skills subjects. It is often possible to clarify concepts in a short period of time when teacher and pupil communicate directly. Certain types of diagnosis are personalized and more accurate when the teacher can observe the way a child approaches and works through a problem.

Teacher-Pupil Conferences

Special interests and abilities can be focused on and developed through teacher-pupil conferences. The purpose of the conference will determine its format. Perhaps a child has decided to go into an independent depth study. The first conference with this child might be to develop an outline of what he plans to accomplish. Subsequent conferences would be scheduled as the project develops. While allowing the child to assume the major responsibility for completion of the project, you would continue to act as consultant, helping by furnishing guidelines for organizing information, pointing out weaknesses and strengths, and redirecting the student to new resources for help and information.

Individual Study

A tutorial approach is not the only way to work with individuals. Programmed learning materials can also be very effective teachers. Originally, programmed learning was associated with teaching machines, but educators have come to realize that the hardware, or machine, is not essential to the teaching program.

Essentially, programmed material is designed to advance a learner through a series of small steps to a new understanding. Each concept is broken down into very small ideas which are presented to the student in a logical sequence. At each step the learner is required to answer a question which he has been led to understand. By requiring the learner to respond to questions, programs ensure that the learner is actively involved while learning. Each answer is immediately checked against the answer given in the program. This immediate knowledge of results, of knowing whether his answer was right or wrong, is another characteristic of programmed learning material.

One of the most flagrant abuses of this type of material is to expect every child to profit from every program. The teacher's manual which accompanies better teaching programs gives specific information about the program's design. The prerequisite skills needed for success are listed and the objectives of the program are given. New vocabulary words are frequently noted, and an indication of reading ability required of the learner included, along with suggestions for pre-testing and post-testing. By closely matching the readiness of the learner to the prerequisites of the program, teachers can utilize programmed material to help maximize the development of individual potential.

SCHEDULES FOR FLEXIBLE GROUPING

A full blown program of differentiated instruction requires that the teacher assume the role of classroom administrator. Some scheduling problems can be handled by adopting a rotating time block schedule. This type of schedule can best be illustrated by describing a primary classroom situation. With modification this plan can be used by teachers at all grade levels as an intermediate step in adopting more flexible grouping arrangements.

After introducing the basic concept of addition, one first-grade teacher analyzed the learning styles of children in her class. Three styles became apparent. Group A children were ready to proceed with more advanced work. These children had little problem handling the numerals and seldom resorted to counting or manipulations to find answers. The children in group B seemed to grasp the concept of addition but frequently had to count out sets of concrete manipulatives, join sets and re-count to find the answer. Group C seemed to require constant teacher assistance and were unsure of how they might go about finding a solution to a problem. This group would require much more direction in using manipulative materials. Although the groups were heterogeneous as far as rate of learning and level of fact mastery, they were similar in their ability to profit from the particular style of instruction.

Since 40 minutes was the time normally devoted for math, she decided to extend her teaching time to 60 minutes, but to include one 20-minute "listening period" for the children during this hour. By rotating the groups through three types of learning activities, she was able to spend more time with individuals and actually spent no more time than she formerly had on math and a listening activity. Her tape recorder was called into service to do some of the story telling she had formerly done. Each listening activity served as a basis for the whole-class activity which followed. Members of each group had been broken down into matched pairs of children. Each team worked cooperatively to solve the day's assignment. The teacher stayed close to the group, observing the way different pairs approached problem solving and keeping herself ready to assist a team when extra help was requested.

Children in group C were given more teacher direction and support through the acquisition of each skill. A varied diet of concrete learning experiences was provided at every level. Changes in grouping were made when individual children developed in their ability to work independently. Each group spent 20 minutes with the teacher, 20 minutes in a related follow-up activity, and 20 minutes with the teacher-on-tape listening activity. Figure 3-1 shows how groups were rotated during this 60-minute period.

While basically a modification of the standard three-groups approach to reading, this teacher's adjustment in teaching strategy based on learning style, made this an ideal way for her to begin to differentiate instruction.

The teacher of a heterogeneous interage class of intermediate level children found a different plan workable. An hour was set aside each day for work in mathematics. Children worked alone or in small groups on self-pacing math materials. Part of each hour was devoted to conferences which were scheduled with the schedule being written on the chalkboard. Below the written schedule children signed up for extra help from the teacher. Children who shared an area of common difficulty might receive help in a group conference. Records of mastery were kept and children were encouraged to first seek help from a child who had already mastered the level which was giving difficulty. On another day a subgroup might be formed because the teacher had determined a common readiness to undertake a new concept. Groups were formed whenever children were alike in some way that seemed to ensure their profiting from similar experiences. Groups rarely stayed together for more than a few days or weeks.

Part of each math hour was left unscheduled. During this time the teacher walked among the children as they worked through individual math prescriptions. Each child met with the teacher once a week to plan a contract of work to be accomplished that week. When this math contract agreement was fulfilled, an individual student was free to pursue any independent activity he desired.

By adjusting the contracts to individual needs and interests, each child was permitted to earn time to do something he really wanted to do. With increasing frequency the free choice activity was more math.

Sample Plan Using Rotating Time Block Schedule for Math Groups

10:00 - 10:20	10:20 - 10:40	10:40 - 11:00
Group A	**Group B**	**Group C**
Work independently through learning materials. Teacher available for consultation and individual evaluation.	Work in matched pairs on daily assignment. Teacher available for help and group evaluation.	Meet with teacher for daily group instruction and short period of individual follow-up activity.
Group B	**Group C**	**Group A**
Work independently on follow-up assignment based on prior day's work.	Work in small teams to solve problems posed in simple work sheets.	Work in math activities designed to develop computational speed. Math games, flash cards, etc.
Group C	**Group A**	**Group B**
Listen with headphones to a taped story which serves as the basis for a later whole group discussion or follow-up activity in a subject other than math.		

Time with teacher available to the group.

Math follow-up activity.

Listening Activity.

Figure 3-1

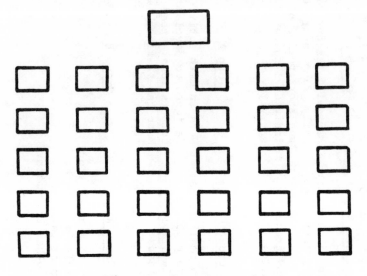

Classroom Arrangement A
Figure 3–2

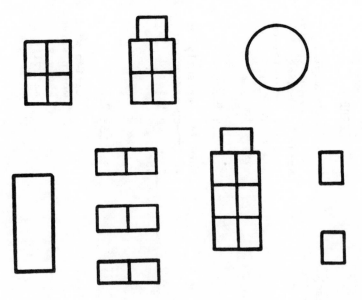

Classroom Arrangement B
Figure 3–3

To be effective, grouping should be flexible. There is nothing sacred about the composition of any subgroup. Once the purposes for which the group was formed are accomplished the group can be disbanded. There never was a homogeneous group —only children who are somewhat alike in some way. Whenever we do manage to get a group together, the reality of human difference will soon make some children shoot ahead while others seem to stand still. As you move toward more flexible grouping patterns you will find many ways to schedule time for individualized instruction.

Organizing the Classroom for Flexible Grouping

Thoughtful arrangements of desks and materials can facilitate your work with children. The floor plans in Figures 3-2 and 3-3 each require the same square footage. Each implies the type of instruction which might take place within such a room. Rows of desks facing the teacher set the stage for the teacher dominated, undifferentiated learning situation. Desks arranged to serve individual needs will serve a variety of purposes, and will be arranged to facilitate different kinds of learning activities. One or two tables might be used for small group discussions, interests, or projects. A single desk might be used by a single child working in a teaching program or as a station for conferencing or tutorial instruction.

Children might move their desks together to form a listening group, or in pairs for teamed activities. For some testing and group screening activities the desks might be rearranged in rows. The types of activities going on in a room will determine the arrangement of desks. Children should be trained to move desks and chairs without unnecessary noise and confusion. When possible, have empty desks clustered and allow children to move these desks for small-group work rather than moving their own desks.

Guidelines for Grouping

Remember that no one grouping pattern will work for all learning situations.

Let the nature of the activity determine the grouping patterns you adopt.

Be flexible—change the group's membership whenever individual members who compose the groups would benefit from the change.

Cluster children on the basis of learning style whenever possible.

Provide for differences within subgroups.

FOUR

Using Pupil-Teams
in the Program

Pupil-team activities provide an excellent starting point for the teacher interested in individualizing instruction. Pupil-teams are teams of two or more pupils who work cooperatively on an assigned task. The use of pupil-teams permits you to work gradually from a traditional "whole-class" approach to a more highly differentiated program. At first you could assign activities where all of the teams work on the same task. This serves as a necessary training period for the pupils, allowing them to feel comfortable with the new way of working, and provides you with time to get acquainted with the basic types of pupil-teams. You will want to note which pupils seem to benefit most from this style of learning. As you become familiar with the several types of pupil-teams, and the kinds of activities which can be used with each, you will begin to realize how many variations can be played on the basic themes.

How do pupil-team activities differ from other, more traditional, kinds of classroom methods? Some of the differences you will notice right away; some are more subtle. The children are encouraged to compare answers and to study each other's papers. The nature of the tasks requires that the pupils talk to each other. These things are immediately obvious as "different" if you have worked largely in whole-class situations. The use of pupil-teams takes advantage of the ability of children to help each other to learn. Team endeavors encourage independence and self-reliance and make possible a high degree of self-evaluation. These subtler things become apparent more gradually.

The number of pupils on a team and the criteria for selecting teammates will vary with the purpose and nature of the activity. When the task involves work in a skill area, such as recognizing initial consonant blends in phonics or addition of like fractions in math, teams of two are recommended. The partners should be chosen so that they are as similar as possible in the skill area to be practiced. In this way they will both be able to benefit from material of the same level of difficulty, they will feel comfortable with each other, and they will be more apt to work at a similar rate.

When a task calls for a wide variety of types of responses and for divergent thinking, such as planning, discussions, or brainstorming, the composition of the team should be more heterogeneous. Teams of four or five pupils are large enough, yet permit each child to participate actively and frequently.

Some teachers have found that social compatability sometimes serves as a satisfactory criterion for selection of teammates: for instance, when teams are to engage in mural painting or creative dramatics. There are also times when interests could be of prime importance in choosing partners. Depth studies, research and report writing, or book review groups are examples of activities that might call for team members who have similar interests. The two most commonly used types of pupil-teams, however, are the matched pairs for work in skill areas and the random or heterogeneous small groups for activities calling for divergent thinking. We will consider several suggestions of activities appropriate for each type of team later in this chapter.

Pupil-teams will vary in duration. Sometimes you will want to appoint teams for a single, short activity. At other times you may want the teams to continue working together for a longer period of time until a certain series of related activities is over or until a given set of instructional material has been completed. There may also be times when you will want certain teams which are capable of working independently to continue for an extended period with only occasional direction from you.

Some pupil-team activities require instructional materials and others need little more than oral directions. Oral directions would probably be adequate for starting teams on a search for illustrations of "ways we use electricity." Most tasks in skill areas such as in reading, spelling, and mathematics will require instructional materials. For example, you might use a worksheet of some kind for a team needing practice in spelling words with suffixes. Such materials should be selected or designed and made so as to be highly self-directing, with instructions easily read and interpreted by the children who will be using the materials. Answer keys or teachers' manuals should be provided for each team so the material is also self-correcting. This enables a team to know immediately if its responses are satisfactory. When the activity involves planning, brainstorming, or discussion, oral directions or short lists of guiding questions are usually all that is necessary to get the teams under way. Since the activities engaged in by pupil-teams stress learning, you will want to make other arrangements for periodic evaluation. These evaluation materials would be administered to pupils individually.

MATCHED PAIRS

Perhaps the most adaptable type of pupil-team for individualized instruction is the matched pair. We have mentioned that this type of team can be used for the practice and application of skills. Some examples of these kinds of activities taken from the areas of reading, spelling, mathematics, social studies, and English are discussed here in greater detail.

Oral Reading

When it is time for a group to meet for oral reading, try organizing the group into several teams of two. Partners in each pair take turns in reading the story aloud to each other. Each child might read alternate pages. In this way, 50 percent of the group is actively involved at all times. Each child has an opportunity to read aloud half of the time. The teacher can still listen to one child at a time, as in conventional reading groups, simply by circulating among the teams, pausing at each for a few moments.

Spelling Tests

Why not let spelling partners dictate words to each other for pre-tests and end-of-lesson tests? This permits testing for several lists of spelling words of different levels of difficulty at the same time. Partners can then work together to check their tests against the original list of words. This technique has the added advantage of giving each child an opportunity to use each spelling word orally in a sentence as he dictates to his partner. The teacher may administer more comprehensive tests periodically which will measure long-term retention of words from several lessons.

Applying Math Skills

Most new math skills need to be introduced directly by the teacher. Learning how to subtract, for example, is an activity that requires much teacher assistance and supervision during the early stages. When children arrive at the point where they have learned the skill and need to practice or extend it, they can work with less teacher direction. At this point, practice exercises can be given to a matched pair of students. Each child would solve an example or problem by himself. The partners would then compare their answers. If they agree, they would go on to the next example. If they disagree, each would explain how he arrived at his answer and together they would attempt to discover and correct the error. After completing a few examples in this manner, they should check with a key or teachers' manual before going on with the assignment. If either or both partners are making frequent errors, they should seek help from the teacher. In this way they will not continue practicing their mistakes.

Map Reading

Two pupils can be given one map and one set of questions to be answered cooperatively from information obtained by reading the map. The partners read the questions, search the map together, and confer about the way to answer the question. You might wish to have each pupil write an answer on his own paper or you might ask the team to submit a single answer sheet. In either case, allowances can be made for differences of opinions about how a given question should be answered. Where each child writes his own paper, he simply records his own choice of answers to the question on his paper. Where both are preparing one paper, both responses are written and each is initialed by the appropriate pupil. Here again, answer keys permit the teams to check their own work.

Vocabulary Classification

When you have several children working from the same basal reader, try pairing them for this vocabulary-building activity. On cards have lists of vocabulary words taken from the basal reader. Select the words for each card so that they can be classified under two or three topics, such as words that tell. What People Do, Things Found in the House, Living Things, Things that Cannot Move, etc. Ask the team to write the words in lists under the given headings. Have the words correctly listed on the back of the card so that the partners can check their work immediately. These cards can be made from ditto masters using 8½″ x 11″ oak tag or card stock instead of duplicating paper. In this way each team may have a complete set of cards and may be allowed to work through the set at its own rate. (See Figure 4-1.)

Checking for Errors

For this activity in proofreading, the partnership should be established so that both members have reached the same level of achievement in the skill to be evaluated. The children should be thoroughly familiar with the objectives for the activity. Are they to be looking for errors in capitalization, punctuation, spelling, complete sentences, paragraph formation, or a combination of two or more of these? Don't ask them to look for too many things at one time until they have had considerable experience with this kind of self-evaluation. More advanced students could be looking for character development or style in a story or for logical development in an article.

Vocabulary* Classification
Figure 4–1

Make two columns on your paper.
Write a title at the top of each.
Put the words in the best column.

	Outside a House	*Inside a House*
butterfly		
bed		
cup		
sun		
floor		
hill		
bowl		
pan		
rain		
room		
ground		
gate		
car		
sky		
fork		
door		
dish		
garden		
window		
stars		

Front of card

Outside a House	*Inside a House*
butterfly	bowl
car	dish
garden	bed
ground	door
hill	floor
stars	fork
sun	window
sky	pan
rain	cup
gate	room
door	
window	

Back of card

___

*Vocabulary words at 2¹ reading level

When the pupils are sure they know what they are looking for, the procedure for approaching the task may be developed. The two children in a partnership will proofread only one story or paper at a time. Both children read one of the papers together. The child who wrote the paper reads it silently, while the other child reads it aloud. Both children point out errors as they read. The errors are circled for subsequent correction by the writer. If there is disagreement about whether something is an error or not an error, the child who wrote the paper makes the final decision.

When one paper has been proofread, they work with the other one, switching oral and silent reading roles. As soon as both papers have been proofread, the partners split up and work independently, each on his own paper. Dictionaries, English textbooks, and other appropriate resource materials should be available for the children to refer to while making the necessary corrections.

Obviously, the children will not find all the errors in a paper. But as their exposure to this type of self-evaluation experience is extended, they will begin to pick out a greater percentage of their errors and, at the same time, will make fewer errors because they become more alert to them as they write the original paper When the teacher wants to make an evaluation of the child's written work, he should collect the papers and do the proofreading himself.

HETEROGENEOUS TEAMS

Many of the activities engaged in by heterogeneous teams of four or five pupils contribute directly or indirectly to a program of differentiated instruction. A few examples are discussed here. These illustrations have been drawn from a variety of subject areas and could easily be adapted to others.

Brainstorming

Brainstorming could be used as an introduction to a new unit or topic of study in science or social studies. No special material or advance preparation is required. Let us use an example from science to illustrate how this activity might proceed. We will use animals as our topic. The class would be organized into random or heterogeneous teams of four or possibly five. All teams are asked to make a list of as many animals as they can think of in a given length of time, say five or ten minutes. One member of each team serves as secretary-reporter. He writes the team's list and reports back to the whole class at the end of the given time.

A complete list is made of all the words listed by all of the teams. Duplicate words appear only once on the master list. The same teams assemble a second time and are given a copy of the master list. They are asked to rearrange the list of animals into groups which are alike in some way. After this has been done, the teams are directed to give each group of animals a title. Then the secretary-reporter from each "buzz" group reports these titles to the whole class. You might find such titles or classifications emerging as Land, Air, Water Animals; Large, Small Animals; Fur, Feather, Scaly Animals; Desert, Forest, Arctic Animals; etc. The teams could be asked to find other ways in which the same animals can be re-classified if you wish to extend this idea. This activity could be used to lead into a discussion of the kinds of animals you will study further.

Show and Tell

Whether it is called Show and Tell or News Time or by some other name, some time is provided at least occasionally by most teachers for children to share experiences and exhibit prized objects. The use of four-, five-, or even six-man teams for this purpose gives each child many more opportunities to participate actively during the sharing time. Allow enough time for each member of a team to participate if he wishes. You will find that even shy children open up more readily when the group is smaller. Somehow four or five children seem less threatening than 30. The teamed activity might be followed by a short period in which two or three children share their news with the whole class. Select different children each time, so that eventually each child will have had an opportunity for this experience, too.

Elaborative Thinking

Today, teachers are asked to help children learn *how* to think rather than to teach them *what* to think. Here is a chance for you to ask questions which have no single right answer. For this activity we are interested in having the children "stretch" their imaginations. We want them to take their thinking beyond the safe, stereotype kind of answer that many questions in school tend to bring forth. To do this the teacher designs open-ended questions that demand divergent thinking. The children, in teams of four, are asked to list as many answers to the questions as they can think of. Imagine the variety of responses you could get to questions like these: What might happen if everything people wrote disappeared in a few hours like disappearing ink? What changes would you make in the world if you had the power to make changes? What might happen if money grew on trees? What problems would we have if suddenly there was no color—just black and white? What would you do if you were the last person in the world? If dogs were able to talk, what might they say to us? Questions can also be designed to be used following the description of a situation, such as is seen in the "Stretch Your Thinking" exercise. (See Figure 4-2.)

STRETCH YOUR THINKING

Tom and Alan had been playing all afternoon in their tree fort. When it was time to leave they put everything neatly away in the storage box, cleaned up the fort, and went home.

The next morning Tom and Alan arrived at the fort right after breakfast. Alan climbed up the ladder first.

"Hey, Tom!" he called down to his friend. "Someone or *something* has been in our fort during the night!"

What could have caused Alan to say that?

Here are some of the responses listed by 30 fourth- and

fifth-grade pupils. There were well over 100 different responses.

Things were out of the box	They saw: a flashlight
There were tracks	a briefcase
The box had been stolen	a dead animal
A board was missing	broken glass
Things were out of order	muddy footprints
A coat was on the floor	a counterfeit
Money was there	machine
Hair was scattered about	a man's wig
There was a strange odor	pad with a code
Their radio was on	on it
The floor was sticky	a $50 check
The roof had fallen in	scattered stones
The door was off	worms in a bait
The rope was cut	box
Perfume was in the air	a bag of marbles
Smell of a skunk	64 written on table
	half an apple
	a dirty sock
	a letter
	a key
	a gold feather

Figure 4-2

These are also effective for the purpose of encouraging creative
writing. Watch for an improvement in the kinds of creative writing efforts children produce after some experiences in elaborative
thinking!

Creative Writing

One procedure for initiating a story writing lesson involves a
pre-writing brainstorming session. The motivating stimulus could
be a picture, a title, a beginning sentence, or a mood. Let us use
just one of these to serve as an example.

The teacher displays on the chalkboard a large colorful picture showing a boy in a football suit, helmet tucked under his
arm, bending over slightly in front of a woman who is using a

needle and thread on the back of his britches. The whole class spends a moment or two telling of the things that are shown in the picture. The teacher then divides the class into four-man teams. Using the picture as a common starting point for all, the teams are directed to consider the following questions. Assume that this picture is one of several illustrations for a story. What kinds of characters might be in this story? In what places could this story take place? What are some of the times when these things could happen? What are some kinds of things that might happen in this story?

After giving the teams a few minutes to "buzz out" the first question, the teacher asks them the second question. By the time they have spent a few minutes brainstorming each question, literally dozens of ideas have been expressed. The children then return to their own desks and write their stories alone. You will be amazed at the variety of situations described in these stories. Some will be about a boy who tore his britches in a football game, of course—the picture calls for some of that. Without the brainstorming, most of the stories would be similar to this. The buzz groups, however, will have set in motion some ideas for stories about Halloween, school plays, costume parties, television programs, and the like. The more often you use this approach to story writing, the more varied will be the story situations your children create.

HOW TO GET STARTED

Four guiding principles for initiating any new methods or materials in the instructional program, apply very strongly to getting started with pupil-teams.

1. Start slowly.
2. State your objectives in terms of what the children will *do*.
3. Get yourself and the classroom organized.
4. Be flexible.

These principles are basic to all good teaching. And using pupil-teams is one of the strategies which can be used in good teaching.

How can we apply these principles to initiating the use of pupil-teams?

During the first two or three weeks it would probably be advisable to plan a small variety of pupil-team activities scattered throughout each week. These activities would be of a one-shot variety. You would probably want to plan for some matched pair activities and some heterogeneous team activities. Your objectives for these first weeks would be merely to have the children try out and react to some of these kinds of activities. The feedback you get from them will guide your future planning. Getting organized at this stage is primarily a matter of deciding specifically which activities you will use, planning how you will space them, and preparing any necessary materials. You will want to be flexible enough to modify your plan if it should seem to be advantageous. You may find you will want to speed up or slow down your schedule of pupil-team experiences or to alter the sequence of activities after you have observed the students working.

Phase two of getting started with pupil-teams might involve training the children to work independently with one or two kinds of tasks or materials. Your objective here · ould be to have the children follow the correct procedure for the assignment. Select two or three activities to incorporate into your program as a part of the regular routine. Such activities don't need to be something that is done every day or without variation, but they should be something that is done frequently enough so that oral instructions for getting organized and getting started become unnecessary. During these early experiences with the pupil-teaming, many of the tasks you assign will be given to the whole class. Plan them so that the level of difficulty will be relatively low. You will want all of your students to succeed in these activities. Always remember that your purpose now is to *train* the children in *how* to work with these routines.

The next step, of course, is to begin to differentiate the tasks according to the needs of the children. You would probably be wise to start with a single subject such as mathematics or spelling or reading. Obtain or prepare practice materials for this subject at several levels of difficulty. Chapter 14 contains many specific suggestions for this aspect of getting organized. When you have assembled these materials, you can have each matched pair work with the material at the appropriate level for that team. By using self-correcting materials, you can permit the teams to progress at their own rates. As the teams work independently, you are free to introduce some new aspect of the subject to a small group who is ready for it. When this group has learned the skill or concept, the members return to independent work in teams and you work with another small group to introduce or review some other part of the subject.

You will want to use other strategies than pupil-teaming for the chosen subject, of course. You will find it important to provide variety and change of pace. And you may find you will want to use pupil-team activities for differentiating instruction in a gradually widening range of subject areas. Start slowly, know what you want to accomplish, be thoroughly ready yourself before you start the pupils in a new area, and be alert to changes that may need to be made in partnerships, difficulty of task assignment, and scheduling of activities.

FIVE

Multimedia:
A Means to an End

A varied educational diet is essential to individualized instruction. Audio-visual materials and equipment provide variety in themselves. When used in combination with each other and with other types of instructional materials, they extend considerably the range of possible approaches to learning. The use of audio-visual instruction has long been a part of most classroom procedure. To adapt its use to the purposes of a program of differentiated instruction, we need to consider the ways in which it can be used with individuals and small groups. More numerous and more purposeful ways of using old standbys, such as films, filmstrips, and records must be sought. We should view all audio-visual materials as untapped resources for direct, developmental instruction. Adapting them to individual needs will involve determining who uses them the purposes for which they will be used, the modifications to be applied to traditional ways of using them, and the accompanying materials or activities which will be used in connection with them.

This chapter is concerned, in part, with discussing the task of organizing a classroom for the variety of activities which will be going on when a multimedia approach is used in an individualized program. Specific suggestions will be given for using audio-visual hardware and software in a variety of ways. Some ideas for using free and inexpensive materials and manipulative devices will also be considered. No attempt has been made to present a complete discussion of the topic. A more extensive treatment of one machine, the tape recorder, is given in Chapter Six. Here we are merely hinting at the infinite possibilities which are available to you when you look at multimedia as a means of providing alternative learning experiences.

Organizing the Classroom

Careful organization and training are essential in reducing confusion during class time. Children will be involved in obtaining, using, and storing a variety of materials and equipment throughout a large portion of the day. You cannot always do it for them. It would probably be wise to spend considerable time in training all children, or a specific group of children, to operate equipment such as filmstrip projectors, tape recorders, and film loop projectors. They should also be trained in the proper care and storage of all materials. The old adage "a place for everything and everything in its place" was never more worthwhile advice. Since children will be responsible for obtaining and returning materials, these should be readily accessible to them and clearly labeled for easy identification.

Mobile Listening Center. Most classrooms do not have a built-in listening corner or a series of wet carrels. You can, with a little ingenuity and effort, make yourself a portable listening center which can be moved to a table or cluster of desks as needed. A wagon, such as a kitchen utility cart or a set of shelves mounted on wheels fitted with a long extension cord, serves as the basis of the mobile unit. A portable record player and a tape recorder should be placed on the unit so that the children can easily change records, thread tapes, and operate the controls. Carefully organized and labeled storage for records and tapes can be designed from cardboard boxes to fit the available space and to accommodate the necessary items. It is not essential to store all your tapes and records on the unit, but you will want to find space for those that are currently being used.

Six to eight sets of earphones will mean that the listening cen-

ter can be used by that many children at a time without disturbing other groups and activities. When children obtain and store
their own headsets there is danger of the cords getting tangled
unless you provide special spaces for storing the sets. One effective way of storing them is to attach hooks to the mobile unit.
Magnetic or adhesive backed hooks can be used on metal utility
carts or screw type hooks on wooden shelf units. To store a head-
set, the child wraps the cord around the headpiece and hangs the
set on one of the hooks. A metal towel bar might be substituted
for the hooks. Another way is to use pieces of cardboard to par-
tition shoe boxes into spaces for individual headsets. This method
requires more shelf space, while the hooks can be fastened to the
back or sides of the unit.

The flexibility and convenience of a mobile unit such as this
will more than compensate for the time and effort involved in
designing and making it.

Viewing Box. Another easily constructed device which pays for
itself in utility is a viewing box. This is essentially a small, rigid
screen inside a shadow box. Individual or small groups of children
can project films, overhead transparencies, film loops, etc. on this
screen. The viewing box is relatively small and lightweight so
that children can easily move and position it whenever they need
it. It can be set on a chair, a desk, a table, a shelf, or even the
floor. When placed at right angles to the wall, the back of the box
can be covered with white paper and used as a second screen so
that two viewing activities can proceed at the same time.

To make the viewing box, select a large corrugated cardboard
box which is almost square and which is not very deep from front
to back. A large size blanket box is satisfactory if it is made of
rigid cardboard. On the front of the box mark off a four- to six-
inch border. This will serve as a frame for the front of the
shadow-box. Cut out the rectangle formed by the inner edges of
this "frame." This makes a large window or opening in the front
of the box. Paint the outside of the box and the sides, top, and
bottom of the inside with a flat black paint. Tempera paint is
not satisfactory for this purpose because it comes off on damp
hands even after the paint is thoroughly dry. Cover the inside
back of the box with white construction paper to serve as the

screen. You may wish to cover the outside back the same way as mentioned earlier.

The viewing box can be stationed more or less permanently or it can be stored and brought out as needed. Various types of projectors to be used with this screen should also be readily accessible to the children. They may be kept on top of movable desks or utility carts so the children can move them up to the viewing box, or they may be kept on stationary shelves or counter tops in which case the children will bring the viewing box to the projectors.

A quick and easy, but less satisfactory, substitute for the viewing box can be made by fastening white construction paper to a small rectangular area of one wall. A viewing box, however, creates less distraction for children engaged in other activities than does the open section of wall.

Filmstrips

We have often been told that items of instructional hardware —filmstrip projectors, teaching machines, computers, etc.—are only as good as the materials which are put into them. It can also be argued that the effectiveness of even the best software will depend largely upon how it is used. For example, a well designed filmstrip introducing the concept of maps and map symbols can be shown to a group in about 20 minutes, which allows enough time to read all the captions. Or it can be extended into a longer experience by pausing to discuss some of the frames and by having children come up to the screen to point out specific things. This would probably be more effective than the 20-minute exposure. However, an even more effective use of this filmstrip might be to have it serve as the core of a series of related map experiences and activities over a period of several days or even weeks. Consider how a single frame from this filmstrip could be used in developing a one- or two-day activity on map scale.

This activity requires a frame which shows an aerial view of a region. Many filmstrips relate this type of aerial view to a map in developing the concept of a map as a kind of plan or drawing which represents an area of the earth. It would be ideal if you could find an aerial view which includes a small town or cluster of buildings, several-roads, a river or two, and possibly a lake or pond.

It would best serve the purpose of this activity to project the filmstrip frame directly onto the chalkboard. If this does not give a clear image, cover part of the chalkboard with white paper and use this as your screen. On the screen draw a four by four grid and label it as shown in Figure 5-1.

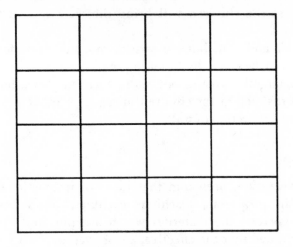

Grid for Map Projection
Figure 5–1

Project your filmstrip frame onto this grid so that the illustration fills the grid space but does not extend outside of it. Let each of the children in your group come up to the board, one at a time, and show how the grid helps in drawing a map, or plan, of the region illustrated. Give each child a duplicated grid drawn in the same proportions as the one on the board. Using as their reference the image of the aerial view as it is projected onto the large grid, have the children draw their own map of the entire region. (If the activity is to span two days, end the first day's work after these maps have been drawn.)

Since the purpose of this activity is to develop a concept of scale, the second phase involves relocating the filmstrip projector farther away from the screen. This time only part of the region shown in the filmstrip frame will fall within the grid which has been drawn on the board. Involve the children in a discussion by posing such questions as these: How much of the original region is now shown on the grid? Has this part of the region actually changed size? Why does it take up so much more space on the board now? How big would our map have to be now if we wanted to show the whole region? How much of it can we show if we make a map of just the part that comes in the grid? Follow up this discussion by having the children make a second map using duplicated grids identical to the first ones. Later they may study their two maps and consider why the maps are the same size if all of the region is shown on one, and only part of it on the other. Use other maps then to relate this to the opposite notion that any given area can be shown on a large map or a small map.

You would not want to plan as elaborate an activity as this for every frame on the filmstrip. Perhaps a sequence of several could be used together for one activity. Probably many of the frames would not lend themselves to more development than a discussion of the presentation in the filmstrip. Some frames you may skip over entirely if they do not seem appropriate for this occasion with these children.

Record Player

Whenever your record player isn't being used for a specific activity, it should be available for children to use, with earphones, just for the sheer pleasure of listening. A collection of story records, children's songs, and instrumental selections should be kept on your mobile listening center. Change the collection periodically to ensure continuing interest. Some favorites may need to be kept longer than others. Ground rules about when and how much a child may use the record player must be established, of course. You will want to do this in such a way that all children will have opportunities to enjoy unstructured listening experiences.

There are available commercial records which contain phonics skill exercises, drill in arithmetic, historical dramatizations, and other curriculum oriented listening activities. These could be located at the listening center for children to use when they feel the need or desire. You might also give specific record assignments to some children from time to time when you feel they would benefit from them. Sets of story books and records can also be purchased. These permit a child to follow a story in the book as he hears it read on the record. If you can obtain some sound effect records, they can serve as interesting jumping-off places for spontaneous creative writing.

In addition to these more or less informal ways of using the record player, you will also find many ways to plan more structured activities around it. For instance, you might have a small group of interested students use it to help them plan and prepare "poetry reading." After reading widely in poetry books and anthologies they would match up some poems and music. This could be done by choosing the poems first and then listening to instrumental records as they silently read the poems to find a musical selection that seems to set the right mood for a poem. Or a long playing record with several selections could be chosen and poems found to fit the moods of the music. This matching of poems and music should be followed by rehearsals for the poetry reading. Each poem would be accompanied by its musical background as it read aloud by one child or by several in a choral speaking fashion. When the program has been perfected it may be presented to the rest of the class or to another class. You may want to make a tape recording of the program. The tape could then be added to your listening-for-pleasure collection.

Films

Films have long been used for providing vicarious experiences, enriching background, and for giving an introductory overview or summary of a unit of study. Such uses of films are worthwhile and often necessary, but you will find that in individualizing classroom activities you will usually not need to use a given film with all children. Children who have had many firsthand experiences similar to those shown in the film will not need the additional exposure. They might spend some time in other pursuits more worthwhile for them. There will also be many times when the whole class will not be engaging in the same study or unit. In such cases it would probably not be appropriate for all to experience the overview or summary film which might be used for those involved in the study.

There are many ways in which films can be used to help you individualize your program. Many of them would be planned for small groups of varying sizes. There might be occasions when a single child would use a film to serve a necessary or worthwhile need. In all cases the needs and interests of the children and the purpose of the activity would determine who would use a film and how.

Taking Notes. A small group of children engaged in preparing a project or report on a given topic might use a film as a source of information. A little advance preparation will provide them with a direction for the activity and a built-in opportunity to practice the skill of taking notes.

The children could compile a list of questions about the topic —questions they feel are important for them to answer in order to carry out their project. It might be wise to limit the questions to about four at first to avoid confusion during the note-taking process. Each child could fold a sheet of paper into fourths and write one of the questions at the top of each section. When the film is projected into the viewing box he would jot down notes in the appropriate section of his paper as pertinent information is given. A group conference after the viewing will permit the children to share their findings and decide on the best way to incorporate the information into their project.

Making and Applying Generalizations. A few children who have given evidence of a developing ability to make generalizations and to apply them, might benefit from an opportunity to practice this skill. Give them a film which you plan to use later with another group. You may plan to use it later to help develop some concept—for example, a film on farming might be used to develop the concept that machines make a farmer's work easier. Ask one group to preview the film for you. Have them prepare a list of questions which will help the children in the next group lead up to this idea or concept. When they have prepared the questions, you might feel it would be a valuable experience for them to explain to you just how these questions can be used to develop the concept. You might even feel that they would be able to help you with the subsequent presentation.

The second group could then be asked to notice some of the machines used by farmers in the film. After viewing the film, they could meet with the children who compiled the list of questions and discuss them. Then you might meet with the group and have them summarize what they talked about in their discussion.

In designing such a series of activities, you would be using a single film as a way of providing different opportunities for different groups of children.

Reconstructing Sequence. The same film on farming might be used in still another way. It could provide semi-concrete experience in finding sequence for some children who have difficulty with this skill. Select a portion of the film which describes an operation involving several steps, such as planting and caring for a certain crop or harvesting a crop. Prepare a set of cards for each child who will participate in this activity. The set should contain a card for each step in the process with a description of the step written on the card. Before viewing the film the children would spread out their cards and talk about what is written on each one. They should know that they are to put them in order, according to the way the farmer follows the steps, as they see it being done in the film. It is not necessary to show the entire film for this exercise unless the sequence requires it. After viewing, the children may compare the sequences they have arranged. It may be necessary to see the pertinent portion of the film a second and even a third time in order for all children to be satisfied with their sequences. This self-evaluation is well worth the time it takes, and it is after the child has satisfied himself he is right, that the teacher should point out (and illustrate with the film again) any errors.

Pupil-Selected Films. There are often times when it is appropriate for children to select the films they would like to see. The children, described earlier, who are searching for information for a project or report would probably like to make one or two selections from a list of films which are suitable for the maturity of the group. A child who becomes interested in a specific topic through his casual exposure to it in some other experience, might like to find out more about it by choosing a film to view. This is really a variation on finding library books on the subject.

A group of youngsters needing more opportunity to practice social amenities, could engage in a project centered around the selection and showing of a film strictly for entertainment. You might have them plan a little theater "World Premier" of a film which they choose. Each child could invite, by written or oral invitation, one guest from some other room. The other children in your room could also be invited, giving additional opportunities to extend gracious invitations. On the day of the performance, each child having a guest from outside the room should greet his guest at the door, introduce him to the teacher and any children he doesn't know, and make sure that he is included in pre-show conversation. An after-show social time may also be planned.

Overhead Projector

The overhead projector is more than an illuminated blackboard which allows you to write on it while facing the class. You are missing much of its potential value if your use of this machine is limited to writing on it and projecting seatwork exercises from it. Put it to use doing things for you that would be more difficult or less effective to do without it.

Use it to enlarge samples of a child's handwriting so he can analyze how to improve it. Make the transparency directly from samples of the child's work. The child will find it easier to identify errors in formation of letters, uniformity of slant and spacing when the sample is projected and enlarged. Let him compare later samples to evaluate his own improvement.

A transparency can provide the stage set for a puppet show with children using small construction paper dolls fastened to pipe cleaners to serve as puppets. The set is projected onto a screen and the paper doll puppets may be laid right on top of the transparency to project an enlarged silhouette. They may be moved about by means of the pipe cleaners. Or larger puppets may be held up directly in front of the screen.

Encourage children to make transparencies as illustrations for some part of an oral report they are preparing. One fourth-grade girl made a four panel overlay depicting the growth of the Saguaro cactus for part of her oral report on the Arizona desert. Each panel showed the cactus plant at a different stage of development from the time it was barely more than bud size until it was fully grown and 50 feet tall. The overlays were designed so that the four figures illustrating the growth pattern lined up side by side on the screen. The drawings were kept in scale, and a small cardboard figure, also cut to scale to represent a six-foot man, was placed on each panel successively during the oral report to serve as a referent for visualizing the size of the cactus.

There are several benefits to be derived from having children use the overhead projector in this manner. Perhaps the most obvious is that it makes the oral report more lively and interesting. Making the transparency also helps the youngster presenting the report. It requires a search for specific data in order to plan the transparency; it assists him in organizing his thinking about how to explain the point he is trying to make; and it takes the place of notes while he is actually giving the report. It also makes oral reporting more fun!

Language Master®

This machine is especially effective for use with one child at a time. It is ideal for developing and practicing auditory awareness and discrimination. Some ready-made programs are available, but to ensure meeting the specific needs of a given child, you will probably want to design and prepare short programs or "practice packages" of your own. To do this you will need several blank cards of various lengths. We shall consider how two such practice packages might be developed.

A child who is able to "underline all the words with the *long a* sound" in a workbook exercise is not always able to distinguish between the *long a* and *short a* sound in spoken words. Nor is he always able to apply his skill in the visual identification of *long a* words to the ability to pronounce them correctly. In preparing a program for him, the teacher would want to concentrate on two things: (1) auditory discrimination and (2) the child's oral

---

® Registered trade mark

pronunciation of *long a* and *short a* words. A set of the shortest blank cards will serve these purposes. The same set of cards can be applied to each objective when used in different ways. At the top of each card write a pair of words, a *long a* word and a *short a* word such as *cap, cape* or *blade, fast.* On the tape, record the correct pronunciation of each word. At first the youngster might merely read the words silently (or whisper them) as he hears them pronounced correctly. Another time he might pronounce both words himself and then listen to the correct pronunciation to check himself. Later the tape may be erased and the correct pronunciation for only one of the words recorded. This time the child listens to the pronunciation and points to (or copies) the word he thinks is being spoken. To permit him to check himself, the correct word may be printed on the back of the card. Several cards like this may be set aside so that he does not have an opportunity to use them in his practice. These will provide him with materials for self-testing when he thinks he has mastered his task.

Another child might need to improve his speed in mental arithmetic computation. A practice package could be designed for him using longer blank cards. Nothing needs to be written on the front of these cards. Two-, three-, or four-step mental arithmetic problems can be recorded on the tape. After a pause, the answer may also be recorded, or it may merely be written on the back of the card. The amount of time the child has for mental computation is limited if the answer is recorded but is unlimited when the answer is given on the back of the card. The problems recorded on the cards might include some like the following.

> "Three times four" (*pause*) "plus three" (*pause*) "divided by five." (*pause*) "The answer is three."
> "Two times three" (*pause*) "times four" (*pause*) "divided by three" (*pause*) "minus two." (*pause*) "The answer is six."
> "Four plus seven" (*pause*) "plus eight" (*pause*) "plus five" (*pause*) "plus nine." (*pause*) "The answer is thirty three."

Single Concept Filmloops

Continuous filmloops are designed to develop one concept and are often referred to as single concept films. Although a teacher's guide usually accompanies each filmloop, some additional teacher preparation may be desirable to develop study materials which will guide certain learners to a greater understanding of the concept.

To design these materials, first view the film and study the teacher's guide. List all the things which are easily recognized and which serve as the foundation for development of the concept. Change your list into questions which will require the learner to "see" all the necessary details. Review the film and formulate additional questions which will require the learner to make inferences about what he has recognized in the film. Structure your questions so that each child who will view the film is led to stating (in his own words) the concept developed in the loop.

One fifth-grade teacher wanted to develop the concept of the variety of structures used as dwellings in Middle America with a group of children engaged in an investigation of Latin America. A filmloop was selected which showed many types of homes and families which, though sharing a common locality, were vastly different.

The children were each given a list of questions to guide them in their first viewings. For each of the nineteen examples of homes shown in the filmloop, questions were asked which required the viewer to notice detail. For example:

SCENE I
1. What materials were used in the Guatemalan Indian homes?
2. Do these homes have electric lights?
3. Does it snow in this part of the world? What clues did you find to make you answer this way?
SCENE II
1. How many stories tall is the apartment building?
2. What kinds of materials do you see which are also used in your home?

Other questions such as these were asked for each of the additional scenes. Then a few final questions were asked to guide the children in making a generalization.

1. How many different kinds of homes did you see?

2. Why are the homes different from each other?
3. Write a paragraph which tells about the homes of Middle America.

Free and Inexpensive Materials

When does a handful of pebbles become an instructional material? When a child has his own 6 x 9 manila envelope of pebbles to use as manipulative material in math. With it he can concretely illustrate that seven means one more than six, that twelve take-away four leaves eight, that one-third of fifteen is five, or that three sets of eight use twenty-four. Commercially designed counters are nice, of course. They are more colorful, for one thing, but they are also more expensive. You may find it necessary to use pebbles, or buttons or bottle caps or some other similar material, if you wish each child to have his own set.

Assume a spirit of adventure about finding and adapting readily available free and inexpensive materials to meet some instructional needs in your classroom. It is certainly challenging and it can be fun. Let the children in on it, too. The need for material to be used for a specific purpose can provide the children with a real live problem-solving situation in which to analyze and select from possible alternatives. It is entirely possible that they might also come up with a better solution to the problem than anything you could think of.

Pictures. One teacher who had a group of children needing more opportunity in writing their ideas clearly, used a set of four large mounted pictures as the basis for an experience in written expression. Each picture was a winter scene of a brook in a wooded setting. There were many similarities among the four scenes, but each had some unique features. The children were asked to study the pictures carefully and to mentally select one of them to write about. The task they were given was to write a paragraph or a poem which described the scene in that picture. After the descriptions were written, the children took turns exchanging papers to see if they could match the correct scene with each written description.

Manipulative Materials. Paper clips and safety pins were used in another room to give the pupils concrete experiences in subtraction calling for regrouping, or "borrowing." Each pupil in the group was given a thousand paper clips in a small carton. The carton contained ten boxes with one hundred clips in each box. The paper clips from one of the boxes were separated into piles of ten. They were then bundled together on safety pins—ten paper clips to each safety pin. The ten bundles of ten clips were then returned to the box. A second box was dealt with in the same manner except that one of the bundles of ten was left loose and one of those paper clips was removed. The child now had nine boxes of one hundred paper clips, one box with nine bundles of ten clips, and nine loose paper clips or a total of 999 paper clips. In working with these materials, the loose paper clips were referred to as "ones," the bundles as "tens," and the boxes as "hundreds."

The children were given orally, many very simple problems to solve before getting into the regrouping aspect. For two or three days they worked on such problems as "put 368 paper clips on your desk." (Three boxes, six bundles, and eight loose clips.) "Take away 42 of the paper clips. How many do you have left?" Then, without advance preparation, the teacher asked them to put 473 paper clips on their desks and take away 35 of them. Careful observation of how the children approached this problem revealed that one or two quickly saw the need to take the clips off of one of the safety pins and add them to the three loose ones on the desk (regrouping). Others pondered and tried various unsuccessful manipulations. Still others gave up immediately and wanted the teacher to show them how to do it. When the teacher suggested that they try to figure out something that would make it possible for them to solve the problem, they began to turn to each other for assistance. They watched each other's attempts and discussed possibilities until all had either discovered the need for regrouping or copied someone who had.

Those children whose insights into the structure of place value had enabled them to discover or "see" this for themselves needed far less additional practice with the manipulative materials than did the other children. Those who merely imitated, required many more concrete experiences before they were ready to attempt the transfer to the more abstract paper-and-pencil subtraction examples. Thus what had started out as one math group had to be reorganized within a few days. Flexible grouping!

SIX

The Tape Recorder: A Second Teacher

How often have you wished there were two of you in your classroom? Who knows better than you the frustration of not being able to get around to every child? Assume now that you have diagnosed the learning needs of your class and the individual children. You know the tremendous job ahead. There just isn't enough "you" to go around, but there can be a second you, a tape recorder.

Think of all the ways you use your voice as you work with children! The stories you read to them, the spelling tests and sentence dictations, the oral directions which are essential for workbook pages and achievement tests. If these were all available on tape you could work "live" with one group at one level and have the "taped you" work with a different group at a different level.

An additional advantage of taping is the factor of recall of teacher effort. Once a tape is created for a specific educational purpose, it can be stored for unlimited future use. Ideally you could prepare a library of taped lessons on every level and for every skill. Overwhelming as it may seem at first, there are some practical ways to begin building such a tape library.

Story Tapes as a Beginning

As you read the next library book to your class, turn on the tape recorder. Label the finished tape with the book's title. You now have your first listening activity tape. We have found that most older children like to "just listen" again to a wonderful book like *Charlotte's Web* or *Winnie-the-Pooh*. As one group listens, the teacher is free to work with another individual or group. Beginning readers enjoy listening to the taped teacher read easy trade books as they follow along. Your adult skill with appropriate vocal dynamics can enhance the simplest story. These stories can be reheard as the child desires, and serve to develop a background of language experiences.

When recording stories, trade books, and tape lessons, a signal can be used to tell the student when to turn or you can simply give the direction orally. The final direction is always "Please stop the tape recorder now." Children's understanding of the terms "good oral expression" and "pausing for punctuation," will be better as a result of this type of listening experience.

Building a Tape Library

Ideally tapes could be prepared for many teacher-directed activities which are apt to be repeated. If we truly differentiate our programs, children will need testing on their own levels and at their own rates. Not every child would be ready for the same test on the same day. Here again don't expect to have everything done at once. Instead, start to record as you give the next spelling test. Record the directions for end-of-the-book tests as you give them. Record your voice as you dictate sentences for children to write.

This may sound like more tape than you can possibly store, but there are some ways to get around this sensibly. First, buy a good middle-grade tape in large reels. Cheap tape doesn't erase well and some taped lessons will be erased after one or two uses. Second, buy many inexpensive small empty reels. These are often packaged in small boxes intended for mailing. In this way you can use the tape in any quantity from the large reels, cut the tape at the end of each recording session, and wind the lesson on a small reel. You would then have easy to use separate tapes for each taped lesson. These can be easily stored by labeling each small box and storing the small boxes of tape in shoe boxes labeled by subject.

Every time you record yourself directing or guiding children you are really packaging your "second self," ready for the next individual or group requiring this type of directions.

Here are a few suggestions which have been found effective. Use them as a guide to stimulate your own creative thinking about uses for the tape recorder.

1. Prepare math drill tapes; the script might go like this: "I am going to read some number sentences to you. We will be working for speed today, and trying to discover which facts are giving you the most trouble. Listen to the problem. Write your answer as quickly as you can. If you don't know, leave the space blank. After three seconds I will give you the correct answer. Check your work. Remember this is not a test. We're trying to find the number facts that you need to work on."

> Ready? $9+4=$. (*pause for three seconds*) The answer is thirteen. $9+4=13$. Ready? $6+5=$. (*pause three seconds again and so on*) Remember that this is a teaching tape, not a testing tape, and that you are trying to develop self-diagnostic learners.

2. Mastery tests for number facts would be designed in the same way, except that here the answers would not be given. Why would this be a better approach to testing than simply giving a sheet of problems?

Here we control the number fact that the child works on and the amount of time he is given to solve it.

3. Some children or small groups of children are capable of a great deal of independent work in reading. Tapes can be made to direct children through a reading lesson. Such a script might go like his: "Turn to the back of your reader where the lists of new vocabulary words are found. (*pause*) Find the set of words for page 16. (*pause*) The first word is 'concerned.' Can you think of a sentence using the word 'concerned'? (*pause*) I was concerned when Betty fell down last week. I was interested and a bit worried. This week our class is concerned about making good plans for a field trip. The boy in today's story is often concerned about the welfare of others."

The tape continues. Each new word is pronounced and given orally in different contexts. After the introduction of vocabulary the teacher, still on tape, can further direct the group to preread with some purpose the entire story. Perhaps there will be a follow-up discussion with the live teacher later that day. Another tape presentation of this type might direct the children to skim the assigned story and write four or five good questions which come to mind as they skim. Again the teacher's purpose will determine the tape's design.

How Do Children Listen?

Earphones and a listening post make a satisfactory arrangement for listening to tapes. This is essentially a series of small speakers (headphones), connected to a central plug, which is then connected to the part of your tape recorder which is labeled "speaker" or, in the newer models, "headphones." Instead of the sound spilling out into the room it is directed into the ear of the student. Before we had earphones, we used our tape recorders without them. Definite standards for using the listening center were set. While the teacher was working with one group of youngsters, another group was clustered in an opposite corner listening to a low volume tape. It was essential for the children who remained at their desks to work quietly. The children understood the reasons for insisting on quiet. They were free to tiptoe to get supplies or to whisper when they had to, and both teaching centers operated smoothly and without interference.

What Kind of Tape Recorder?

Certainly the tape recorder should not be a complicated or expensive one. The fidelity required for voice reproduction is not as high as would be required for music. Many of the standard brand name companies manufacture a school line model. If you're given the choice of having one high-fi deluxe model per school or three medium quality machines, equip three rooms. If the children are to handle the machine it should be sturdy and simple. The best advice on the type of machine to serve your purpose could probably be given by a firm which specializes in electronic reproduction equipment and which carries many brands. The new solid state transistor sets are compact and require fewer repairs.

Casette models are being manufactured by most companies now, and though more costly, might be another satisfactory solution to some of the problems of handling and storing of tapes. A casette tape is packaged in such a way that any child could use the tape without danger of breakage. Both the tape and the take-up reel are encased in plastic. There is no problem of machine threading. Simply drop the package into the machine and you are ready to play back or to record.

Many companies are now producing teaching tapes. Be alert for these as they are introduced on the market. Many times they will not serve the unique needs of your teaching situation, but can serve as an excellent source of ideas. The format of presentation and the methods for student response are usually adaptable at different levels and in different subject areas.

Using the Tape Recorder with Other Media

Listening-viewing centers combine prerecorded material and filmstrip or slide visuals. Groups of children can view the projected image while listening to the commentary which you have prepared. When you want the viewer to turn to the next visual, simply direct him orally to "Turn to the next frame" or "Change to the next slide."

Filmstrip-Tape Combinations. Prepare taped material as you view the filmstrip. The printed material may simply be read to the children frame by frame without any additional comments. Primary grade children enjoy stories presented in this way and may retell the story for chart reading activities. At the intermediate level tape-filmstrip presentations are ideal in content areas which require a high level of reading ability. Better readers can be taught how to record the text and the student-made tapes can be used by less able readers.

You may want the children to respond to questions which you ask. A sample script might run like this.

"Turn to the first frame. (*pause*) The early settlers brought many of their Old World possessions to their homes in the New

World. Can you find examples of these Old World possessions in this picture? List all that you see. When you have finished, turn the tape recorder on again and go on with the lesson."

Children will need some instruction before working with lessons which require them to stop and start the tape recorder. Care should also be taken to allow a long pause on the tape between the end of one section of a lesson and the beginning of the next.

Another tape-filmstrip lesson might be designed to lead the viewer through two or more viewings. The first viewing might present the content material of each frame, while a second viewing would embellish upon the ideas presented with the first viewing.

Slide-Tape Combinations. Slides, professional and amateur, have the additional advantage of being versatile. Each can be viewed in any order the teacher desires. A good slide-tape lesson might use only two slides which are flicked back and forth as children compare and contrast the specific attributes of the concept you are developing. All the suggestions for filmstrip-tape lessons can also be used with slides.

The variety of pictures which can be used is far wider than is available on filmstrips, and you can edit those slides which will best develop the ideas you plan for the lesson.

Encourage children and fellow teachers to share their vacation slides with you. They may allow you to have a copy made of any especially worthwhile slide. Special lenses are available which allow you to take excellent slides of magazine pages. It may be necessary to obtain permission to reproduce such material. When processed, these slides look exactly like the original picture. Museums sell collections of slides which are ideal for adaptation into listening-viewing lessons and which are low in price.

THE TAPE RECORDER AS A LISTENER

Think of how often you listen to the voices of children in order to learn from them how well they are doing. Children answer questions. They tell us what they like or dislike. They tell us what they don't understand. Often their greatest joy is to have us listen as they read. Unfortunately, we have only one pair of ears —unless we enlist a tape recorder to listen for us.

1. Have children read orally to you on tape following a definite format The child introduces himself, tells the name of the book he has chosen, and the pages from which he is reading. Such a tape might run like this: "Hello Mrs. Smith, this is Dewey. I want to read a story to you from *A Hen in a Fox's Den.* It begins on page 68." The child has been trained to use the recorder, and when he has finished recording he leaves the book with his tape. As you listen to the recording after school you might follow along in the text and make notes about Dewey's strengths or weaknesses. You will also have something to talk to this child about in an informal way. What did he especially like about that story? Did he enjoy the illustrations? Perhaps you might suggest another similar story or a poem on the same subject. Children are motivated to read when they know someone is interested.

2. Oral book reports are good. Again there should be a check list of points to be followed, which the teacher designs to meet her own criteria of what information should be included in a book report. The child introduces himself and goes on, responding to the questions on the book report check list. The child can usually express himself much more vividly when not tied down by the act of writing. Children seem much more eager to read and report, and many more will be motivated to read trade books. Most written book report situations are boring, if not totally inappropriate for young learners, and may very effectively teach children to hate books.

Tapes as Records of Progress

Have a tape for each child to add to over the year. A child's growth in oral reading is thus made much more apparent to him and to his teacher. Parent conferences can be more meaningful when this type of record is available for comparison and evaluation.

Use tapes as a record of a group's ability to work together. When working with heterogeneous 4-6 man teams it is possible to evaluate the quality of interaction within one group and to guide others with additional questions at the same time. Suppose that you have seven teams working on a series of brainstorming or buzzing activities. As you walk from group to group you listen to the quality and quantity of responses. Some groups will need some further prodding type questions to reactivate or redirect their thinking. This keeps you quite busy. Leave your other ears, your tape recorder, with one of the groups and record all of that group's session. Label your tape with the names of the team members, the activity, and the date. You can learn much about the abilities of individuals within the team. Who assumes a leadership role? Who participates shyly, slowly or infrequently? Are some members squelching the ideas of others? Free of the demands of total-class needs, you have time to listen reflectively to the way these children interact.

SUMMARY

There is of course a *practicum* for every theory. Essentially we are advancing a theory. Tape recorders can be used to do some of the telling and asking, as well as some of the listening, which are components of your role as a teacher. A successful taped lesson, unlike a successful live teaching lesson, can be stored, ready for the next individual or group. When combined with other media, taped lessons provide variety for the learner as well as an approach to learning which is made meaningful through multi-sensory stimuli.

Tape recorded activities discussed in this chapter included the following:

1. Reading stories
2. Giving spelling tests
3. Providing math drill
4. Testing for mastery of math "facts"
5. Introducing vocabulary words
6. Giving instructions for reading activities
7. Guiding filmstrip and slide viewing
8. Recording children's oral reading
9. Oral book reporting
10. Recording pupil progress and performance

Chapter Ten, Guided Listening Activities, includes many additional suggestions for using the tape recorder.

SEVEN

Providing
Opportunity for
Individual Inquiry

Inquiry as a method of teaching and learning is neither new nor highly technical. The differentiating characteristic of an inquiry approach is an emphasis on solutions to questions posed by the learner.

We can analyze the following rather ordinary situation to demonstrate the process of inquiry. Imagine that you wish to locate a specific reference book. You go to the library and ask an available librarian to tell you where to locate the book. Your question is your own tool to get at information which you want or need. Having developed sufficient problem-solving skill to recognize the probable general location (the library), and an appropriate authority (the librarian), you are rewarded when you follow the librarian's directions. You find the book you wanted exactly where you were told to look. Because you had a good idea of what it was you were looking for, you recognize the book when you do find it. These three steps characterize the process of inquiry.

1. Questions are asked which are specific enough to be answered simply.
2. Answers are sought in a manner appropriate to the question.

3. The learner evaluates the answer he has found to determine whether the question has been fully and satisfactorily answered.

If we re-examine the analogous situation described above, we can expand our understanding. Suppose that we enter the library with only a vague idea of what it is we are looking for. All of the librarian's skills and knowledges will not make up for our own lack of focus and direction.

Our ability to question by itself will not lead us to an answer if we lack appropriate problem-solving skills. Imagine that we enter the library again, this time with a good idea of the exact book we want. Rather than seek out the librarian we consult a fellow library user who "looks as though" he might be able to help. After we try this approach unsuccessfully a few times, we might also begin experimenting. As the book we are looking for isn't a well-known or popular best seller, we might look to see which books were used less frequently and limit our search to those which were rarely touched. The analogy might seem extravagant, but the point is that learners must become skilled in the use of authoritative sources.

Evaluation techniques are equally essential if we are to complete the process of inquiry. When we follow the librarian's direction, we are testing the information which she has given us. We know what we are looking for and, having found a book, we check to make certain it is the one for which we have been searching.

This chapter will be devoted to specific aspects of skills development for inquiry. Examples of teaching techniques which capitalize on and develop the skills of inquiry will be given.

Motivation and Involvement

Mothers of very young children are frequently exhausted by a constant barrage of childish questions. Who, what, when, how, why or where seem to precede their child's every sentence. To the toddler the world is exciting; the more he sees the more he wants to know. Much that we learn before entering school is learned through random questioning and experimentation. What happens to most children somewhere along the way which turns them into apathetic and unmotivated people who attend school only in the sense that they are bodily present?

Do we fail to answer children's questions? Do we demand that children's minds function only to answer our questions? Do we secretly hope that our questions will motivate children to learn? How often do we ignore the quality of learner involvement which occurs when children *want to know*? How frequently do we ignore or minimize the importance of noninvolvement in learning situations? Do schools unwittingly tune out the children?

Begin to keep a log of the questions children ask. It need not be elaborate or complete, but it is important that you record as many questions as you can. If you list only those questions which you think are valid or important you will be making premature value judgments and your log will not serve you as well as it might if you reserved judgment. Try to make a note of the way you handled each question. Over a period of time you will see some patterns emerging. Some children will emerge as question askers; some will rarely ask. Some questions will be repeatedly asked and you will have to determine whether there is genuine misunderstanding and inattention, or whether some children are using questions as defense mechanisms. One child might repeatedly ask for directions as a stalling device for work which is too difficult, boring, or totally confusing to him. Another child might refrain from asking questions even when it is essential that he have further direction and help.

Before you can begin to encourage and develop children's abilities to inquire you will need to create an atmosphere which encourages and respects the questions children ask. Begin by analyzing the way you and your class use questions. Focus first on the questions which are being asked.

Developing an Awareness of the Need to Question

If children are taught to read they must be taught to read critically. Most of the teachers' manuals which accompany basal reading series include sets of questions which help children to think critically about what they have read. There are two drawbacks to most of these approaches. The most obvious is that the questions are posed by *the teacher*. Another drawback is the high degree of internal validity of the material being scrutinized. Fiction is designated fiction and factual information is closely researched before publication. The one exception would be in biographical material written for young readers. One series is written in dialogue which no one could remotely hope to prove accurate. As an example, one book contains a section on the boy Columbus. Christopher and his father have long conversations. The accompanying teachers' manual suggests that children be asked what Christopher's father told him. A critical reader would have to answer, "Who knows?"

We are certainly not developing an awareness of the need to question written information when we fail to alert children to the artistic liberty of authors. We reenforce the tendency to believe everything which is read instead.

An exceptionally creative intermediate level teacher was quite concerned about the credulity of his class when they were reading and reporting what they had read in newspapers. He wrote and reproduced the "news release" illustrated in Figure 7-1.

News Release

Sept. 31, 1968

Providence, N.D. (RP)—The people of this town had the privilege today of watching the world's first demonstration of the Dana Drill developed by the Army Corps of Engineers at Ft. Stevenson, N.D. This drill is able to penetrate rock at the fantastic rate of 700 feet each minute. The drill has a cutting edge of pure Calcite, one of the hardest man-made materials. The speed of this drill will allow scientists in the near future to drill hundreds of miles into the center of the earth to explore the inside of our planet.

Present plans call for the adoption of the Dana Drill by the Great Plains Oil Company. The speed at which the drill is capable of reaching oil will reduce to a few minutes what used to take several days or weeks. It will now be possible to cover the entire state with oil wells in just a few months.

The Oil Commission of the North Dakota government is happy to announce that North Dakota will continue to lead the nation in oil production. Governor Meeker of North Dakota was on hand for the demonstration.

Figure 7–1

After the class had read this article silently, the teacher asked standard content comprehension questions. No one questioned any of the ideas which were contained in the article. A small group had been working on a rock and mineral collection and had been using the scale of hardness. Even they failed to react to the statement about calcite drill tips. Next, the children were asked to tell what they had been doing on the date of the news release. Slowly children began to question the article as they recognized the impossibility of the September 31 date. Could this be a simple typographical error or was the whole thing a fluke? Children were encouraged to research independently for substantiating proof or disproof of "facts" they had read in the article.

A unit of study was then prepared around a series of "news clippings." The second in the series is reproduced in Figure 7-2 to illustrate another example of how materials of this type can be designed.

News Release

February 15, 1969

Lexington, Ky. (NP)—Dr. Rosemary Glenn, winner of the Nobel Prize in Archaeology in 1949, has undertaken the excavation of the Daniel Boone Homestead site near here. Joshua Boone, Daniel's father, moved here with his family in 1776 and built a small log cabin. Daniel Boone, the famous frontiersman, was born the following year, the last of eight children. It was here that Daniel Boone spent the first 16 years of his life. Dr. Glenn believes that the great pioneer is buried somewhere nearby, since Daniel died in Lexington in 1798.

The excavations will continue until 1972. Plans are already being made to develop the area into a National Park.

Figure 7–2

The second article was read with a new mental set; children were anxious to find errors and to use all of the school's resources to prove the nature of the inaccuracies they had found.

While this project was under way, some deficiencies in problem-solving techniques became apparent in certain children.

1. Criticizing became an end in itself with no attempt to justify opinions made.
2. Other misinformation or unsubstantiated opinion was of fered as justification.
3. Research skills were lacking and there was little knowledge of where to go for justification of hunches.

The wide range of abilities required an individualized approach. Discussion groups were formed to help children advance skills of critical inquiry. Some children needed help in stating clear questions, in using various sources of information, and in presenting a case when they felt that they had validated a criticism. Small groups were formed as the need arose to develop information-getting skills; use of the card catalogue, almanac, reference books, and occasionally of local authorities at the nearby museum and university.

Helping Children Perceive Detail

You won't have to convince children that detectives are masters of inquiry. Television has portrayed that criminals are trapped by the professional detective's ability to question evidence. You might prepare "clue packages" for your children to use in describing imaginary criminals. Each clue package should be separately wrapped and sealed. Include some of each of the following kinds of items to serve as clues:

1. Receipts of all kinds, sales slips, price tags, theater stubs, ball game tickets, etc. Tags which include size, item, date, price, location, and similar data are best to use.
2. Paraphernalia such as fishing fly, golf tee, clarinet reed, hair curler, directions from hair dye, maps with routes marked, match books and soap from hotels, foreign coins or stamps, bank deposit slips, etc.

Although each four- or five-man team has a different set of clue items, the directions will be the same for all groups. Each group will study the clues and write a description of the criminal who left these clues. Wanted posters can be designed and one member of each team selected to deliver an "all points" bulletin.

The clue packages can be passed to another group for comparison of conclusions. Allow children to discuss their reasons for inferring different information from the same clues.

Using Questions to Obtain Information

Childhood games like Twenty Questions and I'm Thinking of Something that Begins with B, are excellent ways to develop questioning ability. When you couple the idea of questioning games with an evaluation of a tape recording of the responses made during the game, you are structuring a valuable learning situation.

A simplified version would go like this. After telling the children that you will only be able to answer yes or no to any question, turn on the tape recorder. Next say to the children, "I bought something last night; what did I buy? You will have three minutes." At first children tend to ask specific questions.

"Did you buy a dress or a magazine or a pie?" Soon, someone will ask a generic question.

"Did you-buy something to wear? Or to read? Or to eat?" Once an appropriate generic question has been asked the children will quickly get the correct answer. If the children fail to ask the correct question during the time allotted, play back the tape and guide them to recognize generic questions which limit the field of choice.

Other teacher-posed inquiries which can be used to refine questioning ability in children might include these:

I want to take a trip. Where would I like to go?
I am thinking of an animal. What is it?
I'm thinking of a famous person. Who is it?

Insist upon children asking questions in a form which requires only a yes or no answer. When children use the wrong form, ask them to restate their question. If you are unsure of an answer, tell them you do not know the answer.

Developing Conceptual Frameworks for Inquiry

Everything which we seek to define can best be defined by describing the attributes or distinctive characteristics of the item in question. Children can be helped to develop more complete understandings if you teach them to utilize a method which develops an awareness of all of the attributes of any specific thing.

A fifth-grade class was asked to list all of the attributes which characterized discovery. After breaking into heterogeneous four-man teams, each subgroup listed all of the ideas which the members felt characterized discovery and discoverers. A period was set aside to allow each group to report back to the class about the ideas which had been listed. A compiled list was drawn up and discussed. Some ideas were added and others deleted.

The final compilation looked like this.

DISCOVERIES	DISCOVERERS
Something formerly unknown or unnoticed is examined.	People who look beyond the surface of "obvious" things.
Sometimes discoveries change the way people have been doing things to a more positive or time-saving way.	People who seek a better way and have faith that a better way can be found.
They are frequently practical ways of making what was formerly a dream into a reality.	People who work hard to make dreams work.
	People who follow up hunches with experimentation and exploration.
Can lead to other discoveries.	People who build upon ideas of others.
Lead to new ways of looking at truth.	People who challenge the "truth" of currently held opinion.
Do not always lead to improvement of human existence.	People who are often more interested in finding answers than in how the answers will be used by others.

Are achieved through exceptional effort.	People who like to spend time and effort in meeting a challenge.
Are sometimes accidental by-products of other efforts.	People who are alert to other ways to do something or other ways to use information.
Are valuable when human beings have problems which demand solutions.	People who can analyze a problem which must be solved.

When they had completed the list of attributes for each concept, the class worked as a group to compare some famous discoveries and discoverers using the lists as a study guide. Each attribute was restated as a question.

This Attribute—Became—This Question

Something formerly unknown or unnoticed is examined.	What formerly unknown or unnoticed thing was examined?
Sometimes discoveries change the way people have been doing things to a more positive or time-saving way.	What way of doing things was changed in a positive way? Was time saved by the new way? How was the way of doing things changed?

The children were excited when they realized that the study guide questions which they had designed were equally valuable regardless of the specific example they chose to study.

Individual reports were planned focusing on special interest areas but using the same study guide questions. A concept of discovery was developed throughout the unit, and children were led to value conceptual framework in developing their own research reports.

A similar approach was tried in a multiage heterogeneous class of early primary children. The children lacked writing skills necessary for taking notes, and the teacher felt that a free flow of ideas would be hindered if she had to write down all the responses. A tape recorder was used instead. All the children gathered around as the teacher began the first attribute discussion. How is a dog like a cat? The children were familiar with both dogs and cats and ideas flowed steadily. Occasionally one child disagreed with another or strayed to a remembered anecdote about a particular animal. The teacher simply said something about that being interesting but could that statement be made about every cat or every dog? How a dog is different from a cat was also discussed. The next day the group met to formulate the definition of a cat and the definition of a dog. The definitions were highly descriptive and complete.

The teacher replayed the tape for herself and compiled a list of common characteristics for dogs and cats. These characteristics or attributes were listed on a chart.

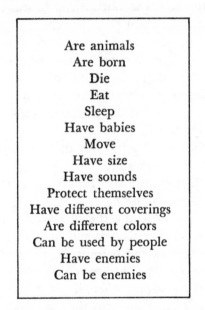

Are animals
Are born
Die
Eat
Sleep
Have babies
Move
Have size
Have sounds
Protect themselves
Have different coverings
Are different colors
Can be used by people
Have enemies
Can be enemies

This list was discussed with the children. The generalizations were related to specific statements which the children had made in the taped discussion.

"Could you use the same list of ideas if you were studying a horse? A fly? Any animal?"

The children thought so. Again each attribute was restated as a question and a class study guide was made. Group and individual studies based on interests continued throughout the year. A concept of animalness was developed and understood by every child in the group.

Formulating and Testing Hypotheses

A clear plastic freezer-type container was distributed to each pair of children in one class. Each container was one half filled with water. A similar kit of items was given to each pair. Each kit had small pieces of various kinds of wood, plastic, paper clips, thumb tacks, pieces of paper, chalk, cork, bottle caps, etc. The first question asked was, "What can you discover with the things which ʸ have given you?"

The answer, "What will happen if you put something in water?" was the only response put on the board. All other answers were accepted as possibilities. The children were then asked what kinds of things they could do to find an answer to the question on the board. The answer "put a piece of wood in water" was recorded only after a specific piece of wood had been named. The statement was changed to a question. "What will happen if the balsa wood is put in the water?" This question was then written on the board.

Next the teacher asked what they thought would happen when the balsa was put into the water.

"I think it will stay on top." This hypothesis was recorded on the board beneath the question.

A quick plan for recording the questions which the pairs formulated, the predicted outcomes and the subsequent results, was discussed before freeing the pairs to begin their experiments. As the children worked, the teacher circulated among the groups asking additional questions. What if you put a paper clip on top of the balsa wood? How far into the water did the piece of plywood sink? What happened to the water level when the plywood sank? How do you know? Felt tipped pens were called into play to mark water level and degree of submersion. As the children worked they were better able to predict outcomes and to hypothesize. This activity carried over through many days. Other materials to test were given to the children as they seemed ready to undertake new ideas. A stopwatch was used by a few children who wished to compare the rates at which various items sank, and simple balances became necessary for proving weight differences.

Group conferences were held at the end of all the experimentation, and children evaluated how they had changed in their ability to make and test a hypothesis.

Another approach was tried in a third-grade class. The children all observed the same phenomenon and then broke into four- to six-man teams to "buzz out" all the questions which the observation had raised in their minds.

For example, after watching candles burn for about three minutes, the buzz groups met, listed their questions, and reported back to the whole class. One member of each team served as secretary-reporter. Each different question was written on the board.

> Would a fatter candle burn as quickly? As brightly?
> What happened to the wick?
> Did you need a wick?
> Did the wax burn?

The questions were then written on strips of paper and displayed on a bulletin board.

Next the children read all the questions on display and each worked with a partner to think of "some ways we could work to find an answer" to any of the questions. Each idea was written on a separate sheet of paper and signed with the names of the partners who had worked on it. As soon as a pair completed a suggestion it was mounted on the bulletin board under the question it was designed to answer. If another pair had already thought of the same method, only the first suggestion was mounted. A schedule of experiments was set up and individuals who thought up the original idea were in charge of each experiment.

Using Living References

Every community has its share of experts. Specialization in any interest area must be accepted as a definition of expertness without such artificial limiting criteria as formal education, fame, or status. A fifth-grade class was fascinated by the art of Japanese brush writing. Knowing that more than one young Japanese family was presently living in the community, the teacher discussed the possibility of having one of these "experts" come to speak to his class.

Before inviting this guest, the class worked in small buzz groups to determine what kind of questions they might ask. The visiting expert would have special knowledge about the writing system to the same degree that any citizen of this country would have special knowledge about our own writing system. Questions about the history and derivation of forms were excluded by applying this criteria. A list of questions was then prepared.

1. When do Japanese children begin to learn to write this way in school?
2. What materials are used when learning?
3. How do you form the letters or words?
4. Could you teach us some easy words?

When the invitation was extended, the list of questions was included in the body of the invitation. The resulting visit was highly informative and pleasurable. By carefully evaluating the kinds of information and help which they might get from this community resource person, children provided for themselves a true experience in utilizing living references.

Second-grade children were studying homespun crafts and tasks of colonial living in connection with an economics centered social studies curriculum. Several women in the community agreed to meet with the children for a discussion of these topics. Classroom planning to determine just what would be covered during the visit was facilitated by a suggested list of activities which the guests felt they could prepare to lead. From the list the class chose to learn about butter making and rug making.

A list of questions which the children wanted to ask was given to the guests well in advance of the visit. Rather than simply giving the answers, these women graciously provided demonstrations and allowed the children to participate in both activities, using antique equipment.

SUMMARY

Some skills of inquiry can be developed in children of any age. As was stated earlier in this chapter, children learn through inquiry prior to coming to school. Children do need guidance in some of the techniques of successful inquiry. Open-mindedness and a willingness to question are perhaps the most important attributes of an inquiring mind. The abilities of idea testing and information gathering are necessary if young learners are to grow through inquiry.

We hear much about the explosion of knowledge and its implication on curriculum content. Although we will continue to be uncertain about what information or what facts children must be taught in order to cope with and contribute to their future, we can be confident that the abilities to formulate questions, to find appropriate answers, and to communicate these findings will continue to serve as valuable tools for lifetime learners.

EIGHT

Oral Communication in an Individualized Program

Walk into any classroom. During the course of a typical day, who will do most of the talking? In the majority of cases it will probably be the teacher. Are we to assume then that it is the teacher who needs the greatest practice in developing his skills of oral communication? Most of us would agree that it is the child who needs the opportunity to build these skills—to be able to state his ideas clearly, to listen attentively to others, to disagree tactfully, and to contribute to but not dominate discussions. But do we really provide these opportunities for children in the classroom? Not if we limit their talking to answering our questions, and not if we plan situations where only one child in a class of 30 is able to talk at one time.

This chapter will consider how discussion groups can be used to meet a variety of objectives in a program of individualized instruction. The composition of groups for specific types of discussion activities and the role of the teacher in working with these groups will be described. There will be several examples of group discussions involving structured sequences of activities as well as suggestions for unstructured discussion experiences.

The ability to work productively with others is a real need in our interdependent, group-oriented society. In preparing youngsters to take their places in this society it is important that the skills of cooperative group participation be developed at appropriate levels of sophistication throughout the educational program. It has also been mentioned that children need opportunities to develop skills of oral communication. All through life, most of our daily communication is oral. Speaking cannot be practiced and improved unless many situa ion permitting speaking are provided. These speaking experiences should not be primarily of a reporting nature. Oral reports have a place in any good program, but they represent a minority of real-life speaking situations and should be given a proportionate emphasis in the classroom.

A program designed to develop skills of oral communication and group participation should consist of a balance of various types of speaking and discussion activities. Whole class discussions are occasionally appropriate when they serve some specific goal, such as initial planning and allocation of tasks to subgroups. Discussion of some topic under study is best handled in smaller groups. Where children are involved in setting their own goals, you will rarely have an entire class engaged in a study of the same topic or the same aspect of a topic. Smaller groups also permit greater involvement in the discussion activity. Oral reports, like whole-class discussion, should serve some specific objective. When a group has broken up into smaller units to distribute the task of finding background information for some project, oral reports to the original group would be very appropriate. Most oral reports serving such real purposes will be given in smaller groups rather than to the whole class.

Small-group discussions will be structured for a variety of purposes. Open-ended discussions will be quite informal in nature and require little, if any, teacher-prepared material. Problem-solving discussions, while task-oriented, should encourage divergent thinking coupled with careful analysis of alternatives. Group discussions can be designed to further concept formation or value clarification. Others may emphasize the skills of group participation. These types of group discussions will require a more structured kind of guidance which may be given in the form of oral or written guiding questions. A balanced program will include some of each type of discussion activity. However, needs of specific children will undoubtedly call for some of them to spend a little more time in one or two of these to give additional practice in certain skills.

As implied here, the needs of the children will often determine the composition of a group. At other times interests of children might serve as the basis for assigning them to specific groups. The nature of a task may also affect group composition. Often in group discussions it is most desirable to elicit a wide variety of responses to stimulate thinking and to provide alternatives to be analyzed. Heterogeneous or randomly selected groups will increase the divergency of the responses. Heterogeneous or interest grouping for discussions also provides opportunity for interaction among pupils who rarely work together in other, more homogeneously structured activities.

The teacher has three main kinds of tasks to perform in connection with group discussions. First, he must design a balanced program with a variety of discussion situations and prepare any guiding questions which will be needed. He must also determine how much exposure to provide for each child in each type of activity and plan for appropriate group composition. Both of these are prediscussion types of tasks. The third task category relates to his role during the discussion activities. In most cases he will not want to assume leadership. This is a role to be shared by the children. The teacher can be most effective circulating among the groups engaged in discussion giving encouragement, asking occasional questions to stimulate or redirect thinking, or making suggestions for a group's evaluation of its progress.

STRUCTURED GROUP DISCUSSIONS

Structured group discussions are those which are designed to foster some kind of end product in terms of the behavior and attitudes of the children. These might include skill development of various types, problem solving, concept formation, or value clarification. The end product of discussions for skill development would, of course, be greater competency in a specific skill. This would require highly structured guidance. In problem solving discussions the end product is a solution to a given problem. Although the teacher provides some guidelines for the discussion, the solution should not be a predetermined "right answer" but should result from the children's analysis of their own ideas. Concept formation through group discussion requires a highly structured approach when the teacher is trying to guide thinking to the formulation of a specific concept. Value clarification leaves the ultimate generalizations up to the child and therefore requires a more open-ended type of guidance. Guidance for these activities would be geared to the skills and maturity of the group. Younger children would be given oral questions one at a time where older children could be given sequences of printed questions. The degree of sophistication of the problem, concept, etc. would also depend upon the maturity of the group.

Picture Study

This activity was designed for a group of fourth-grade students interested in a study of pioneers. You could very easily adapt it to a much younger group or make it more challenging for older children simply by altering the kinds and number of questions and the method of presenting them to the group.

The primary objective for the activity was the development of picture-reading skills. The teacher was interested in having the children (1) increase their awareness of detail in illustrative material, (2) answer questions with information obtained from pictures, and (3) make justified inferences based on illustrations. The development of any concepts about pioneer living was of secondary importance. The teacher was merely attempting to capitalize upon an interest to serve as a focus for the skill-development activity.

Five 9 x 12 pictures depicting various aspects of pioneer living were selected from a portfolio containing over 20 such illustrations. Questions were designed for each of the five pictures so that each question required the application of one of the three skills listed as objectives. Nine children were involved in the activity and were divided into two groups so that each group was as heterogeneous as possible. During a discussion period each group was given one picture and the list of questions designed to accompany it. They were asked to talk about the possible ways of answering each question. A different picture with its list of questions was used during subsequent discussion periods until both groups had discussed four of the five pictures. Then the groups were combined and a quick summary made of the kinds of answers they had found to the lists of questions. During discussion periods the teacher spent some time with other children, and only occasionally needed to encourage one of the groups to consider a greater number of possible answers to a given question or to justify some answer or inference based on the picture. The teacher sat in as an observer on the final discussion with all nine children. This gave her an opportunity to evaluate how well the group as a whole had accomplished the objectives. Individual evaluation was based on each child's written responses to the questions formulated for the fifth picture. Each child worked on this activity independently.

The questions listed were designed to go with the picture illustrated in Figure 8-1.

Figure 8–1

1. Why might this pioneer family have chosen this particular place to settle? Give several reasons.
2. What did the area probably look like when they first arrived? What makes you think so?

3. List all of the things that have been done to make the home and land look as it does here.
4. Rearrange the items in your list. Put them in the order in which you think this family might have done them. (What do you think they would have done first, second, third, etc.?) Why do you think they belong in this order?
5. What tools and implements would they have needed to do all these things? Which of these could they have made after they arrived here and which would they probably have needed to bring with them? Why do you think so?
6. What are some of the ways in which the trees which were cut down have been used?

Concept Formation

A first-grade teacher was planning a social studies unit on trans portation with some of her advanced students. She wanted to develop the ideas that there are many ways to travel and that we select the method we will use according to where and how far we are going. To do this she designed a series of group-discussion activities all based on the same format. A small bulletin board was used as part of her approach. In the center of the bulletin board was a chart with a list of questions. Surrounding the chart were mounted pictures of various kinds of transportation—bus, auto, airplane, motorboat, ship, helicopter, spaceship, etc. Each of these was numbered with a large black numeral. Six questions were listed on the chart.

1. What is it?
2. What is it for?
3. How is it not like some of the others?
4. How is it like some of the others?
5. Where do you go in it?
6. Why is it better for some trips than the others?

On the first day, the group of six youngsters gathered around the bulletin board with their teacher. The questions were read and their meaning discussed in much the same way as a reading lesson might be presented. Then one of the black numerals was replaced with a red one. The children were told that this would be the signal the teacher would use to let them know which way of traveling they were to think about each day. On this first day, the children were to think about the automobile. They were to discuss the answer to each question as it related to the automobile. After the discussion, each child was encouraged to draw a picture to illustrate one of the possible answers to question five. Some of these were then mounted and added to the bulletin board, with yarn running from the numbered picture to the corresponding drawings. On subsequent days a red numeral would signal a different method of travel to discuss and illustrate.

Group Dynamics

Some upper elementary children might profit from a group discussion experience which utilizes higher level skills of group dynamics. Such an experience might call for an analysis of interaction in a group. The children could be trained to keep and read a simple participation chart. The frequency and direction of each member's participation in the discussion can be recorded on the chart by means of lines, showing to whom the child spoke, and arrowheads, showing the number of comments made. A partially completed participation chart is shown in Figure 8-2. When all children in the group have learned how to record participation on these charts during a discussion and to interpret the lines and arrowheads after a discussion, they are ready to undertake an analysis of the interaction within the group.

A highly structured sequence of questions would be designed to lead the group in this analysis. The questions might include, among others, some like these. The children would refer to the participation chart to answer them.

1. How many times did _____ speak to the whole group?
2. Is there anyone who spoke to just one person more times than he spoke to the whole group?
3. Did someone do much more than his share of talking? Why?

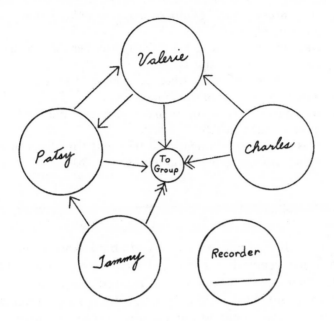

Partially Completed Participation Chart
Figure 8–2

4. Is there someone in the group who did not talk as much as the others? Why?
5. What could you plan to do next time to make sure that everyone has his share of times to talk?

In connection with this interaction analysis, the children might also be led to analyze the role playing that goes on during their group discussions. For this purpose, you might have the group make a tape recording of one or more of its regular discussions. If this is done occasionally for other purposes, too, the children will be more apt to act as they normally do during a discussion. Care should be taken to make the taped discussions as typical as possible by avoiding tension and by waiting until later to tell them how they will use the tape.

Another sequence of questions will guide them in their analysis of the recorded discussion. Since you want the children to analyze the kinds of roles they assume during a discussion, questions like the following might be used.

1. Did anyone in the group keep saying unkind things to someone else?
2. Did someone try to get a quiet or shy member to share ideas with the group?
3. Were there any times when someone said something to hurt another person's feelings?
4. Did anyone try hard to make sure everyone had his share of time to talk?
5. Was there a time when someone could have been more polite in disagreeing with another person?

Problem Solving

In education we are often concerned about motivation. Lesson plan formulas generally recommend some kind of interest-catching introduction to a lesson. When children are permitted to become actively involved in appropriate activities at a level of difficulty which challenges but does not frustrate them, artificial motivation is unnecessary. Natural enthusiasm for learning provides the impetus. In fact, it can provide too much impetus at times. When 30 enthusiastic youngsters are engaged in stimulating learning activities, the noise level may sometimes get too high. This became a problem in one intermediate classroom and the teacher decided to give the children an opportunity to solve the problem themselves.

Since this was a problem involving the whole class, she included every child in a discussion of the situation. A whole class discussion was ruled out since it would permit only one child at a time to speak and might be threatening to some of the shy youngsters. The teacher organized the class into six smaller groups to discuss the problem. She gave each group the assignment shown in Figure 8-3.

During the first discussion period the children considered the questions and compiled the list called for on the assignment sheet. The teacher then compiled a master list of all the starred solutions and duplicated a copy for each child. The groups met a second time to discuss and analyze the suggested solutions. This time each group was asked to draw up a master plan which included all aspects of the best solution they could think of. Again

---

Problem-Solving Assignment

Some of you have said that there are times when the room gets too noisy for you to concentrate on your work. This seems to be a problem that bothers most of us at one time or another. Let's see if we can figure out some of the reasons for the problem and think of some ways we could try to solve it. Think about these things:

1. At what times does the room seem to get too noisy? Why is this a problem?
2. What kinds of activities seem to become noisiest? Is some noise necessary sometimes?
3. What kinds of activities do you feel require quiet times?
4. Are there any changes we could make which would help to keep the noise down?
5. List as many possible solutions to the problem as you can think of.
6. Look over your list and decide which ones would be the best ones to try. Put a star by the best ones.

Figure 8–3

the teacher duplicated copies of the six plans so that all the pupils had a copy of each plan. The third period was devoted to a whole-class discussion for the purpose of arriving at a single plan which would be put into operation. During this whole-class discussion it was decided to incorporate ideas from three of the plans into the final plan. The result was a three-point plan involving a modification in the schedule, a "resolution" for the children, and an "emergency tactic" for times when the other parts of the plan weren't working too well. The ultimate plan is given below.

1. A change would be made in the daily schedule to set aside an hour and a half during the morning as a quiet period. During this time independent activities requiring the greatest concentration would be undertaken. An hour toward the end of the day was devoted to activities that couldn't help but be noisy. The rest of the day was called "medium quiet" time. This was defined as permitting subdued conversation and orderly moving about.

2. Each child would make a concerted effort to control the level of his own voice, and would not reprimand another for being too noisy. Any reminders about being quiet would be made discreetly by the teacher to the child. At the end of the day, each child would rate himself on a three-point scale as to whether or not he had been too noisy during the day. The teacher would rate the classroom as a whole on the same scale and keep a chart of her ratings on the bulletin board.
3. Whenever the noise level was beginning to creep up too high, the teacher would give a warning signal by flicking the lights two times.

This plan was quite successful although some days were better than others. This was to be expected, of course. Occasionally it was necessary to modify the schedule of quiet times and active times, but the need for temporary changes was always explained and the children knew they would soon return to "their" schedule. As a rule children adjust to changes in routine and scheduling if they understand the need for such changes. The teacher felt that this way of resolving the problem was probably more successful than a mandate of her own ideas would have been. Certainly the children benefited from this opportunity to exercise self-control.

Value Clarification

This kind of discussion activity is similar to concept formation. The main differences are in the abstract nature of the value concept and the open-endedness of the final product. Concept formation experiences are highly structured to lead to a predetermined concept. In value clarification, the child is led to consider, from a variety of points of view, some notion such as fairness, trustworthiness, or justice. It is left up to him to form his own conclusions or make his own generalizations about what is fair, trustworthy, or just.

Here are some guiding questions that might be used in a discussion about "honesty."

1. What does *honesty* mean?

2. Should everyone be honest?
3. Are there ever any times when it is all right not to be honest?
4. Tell of some things you know about which were examples of honesty.
5. Tell some examples of things which were dishonest.
6. Could there ever be a time when being dishonest would help someone you love? Explain.
7. What would you do if being just a little bit dishonest would keep you out of trouble?
8. What would you do if being just a little bit dishonest would keep a friend out of trouble?
9. Suppose you saw someone in your class hitting a younger child so that the younger child was hurt quite badly. Would it be honest for you to keep quiet and not tell about what you had seen? What things might happen if you did tell? What things might happen if you didn't tell?
10. Imagine that the person who had hurt the younger child was a good friend of yours. What would you do?
11. Is it possible for you to get into trouble by being honest?
12. What does honesty mean to *you*?

In addition to using such questions to guide a discussion, you might give a case study to the group to read and discuss. The use of simulated situations such as is shown in Figure 8-4, is growing in practice at all levels of education. Such a case study should be designed so as to put the participant in a position of having to make an extremely difficult choice between two or more alternatives, each of which can be supported by some line of reasoning.

UNSTRUCTURED DISCUSSION ACTIVITIES

Some group discussions will require much less teacher guidance than those already discussed. Direction during this more informal type of discussion will come from the children involved more than from the teacher-prepared guiding questions. Often the purpose for the discussion will be quite spontaneous or will come from the children. When the teacher initiates the activity, brief instructions given orally should suffice. Many unstructured

CASE STUDY

Cindy had a dollar bill in her coat pocket. She was to give it to the teacher to pay for her class picture. While she was waiting for the school bus, her hands got cold so she pulled her mittens out of her pockets and put them on. Soon the bus came. Cindy felt nice and warm in the bus so she took her mittens off again. As she stuffed them into her pockets she noticed that her dollar was missing.

"It must have fallen out when I got my mittens," she thought.

Just then Teddy Andrews started bragging about the money he had and began waving a dollar bill around. Cindy knew that Teddy didn't ever have much money of his own. She remembered that he had run over near her and picked something up off the ground when she had been pulling on her mittens. She had looked to see what it was he had picked up, but Teddy turned away quickly and put it in his pocket.

"I'll bet Teddy picked up my dollar and is saying it is his own!" Cindy decided.

Cindy was the last person to get off the bus at school. As she stepped down she saw a dollar bill drop from Teddy's notebook. No one else seemed to notice it. Cindy picked up the dollar bill and stood still, looking at it and trying to decide what to do.

What choices does she have? What should she do? Why?

**Case Study
Figure 8-4**

discussion activities will be task-oriented but the end product will be of a temporary nature. Various kinds of planning activities would be included in this category. The party or exhibit or program being planned will be of relatively short duration. On the other hand, structured discussions such as those described in the preceding section were designed to meet objectives, such as skill development or concept formation, which would in turn serve as a basis for further developmental activities.

The unstructured discussions considered here represent various degrees of task-orientation and informality.

Discussions for Planning

Children like to plan when the plans are being made for something real. Planning for some hypothetical situation or event is artificial and requires extrinsic motivation. There are many valid learning opportunities in planning for real-life activities. Such opportunities cause children to project their thinking forward in time. They try hard to think of every possible need or desired outcome. Planning to accomplish something within the framework of limitations of time, space, or other considerations gives them real child-size problems to solve. Working to carry out their plans often helps them to realize that modifications sometimes have to be made. Children often have unrealistic ideas about how elaborate or extensive or impossible their plans may be, but the experience of trying to put these plans into action helps them to become more realistic. They also learn that planning is not enough; work is required to accomplish what has been planned. Finally, they can realize the satisfaction and sense of accomplishment which comes when an event for which they have planned and worked becomes a reality. And the best part of it all is that it is "all theirs." The teacher didn't do it for them or tell them how to do it.

Parties. Two teachers in the same school used group discussions for planning class parties, but each approached the activity differently. This school traditionally limited classroom parties to four occasions—Halloween, Christmas, Valentine's Day, and the end-of-the-year.

One of the teachers had the activity begin with a whole-class discussion to consider the kinds of tasks needed to be accomplished. Then the children, who were third graders, met in smaller groups according to interests to plan and carry out one specific aspect of the party preparations. One group or committee worked on decorations, another on refreshments, a third on games and activities, and so on. These groups often broke down into smaller subgroups as the children realized the value of distributing tasks. A few days before the scheduled party, the committees reported to the whole class on their plans and the progress that had been made. Time for last minute preparations and arranging of "things" was scheduled for the day before and again for the day of the party. This basic format for party planning was followed for all four party days.

The second teacher, who had intermediate level children, divided her class into four heterogeneous groups. She gave each group complete responsibility for one of the year's parties. After a group had met to discuss plans for one of the parties, they reported to the teacher. At this time they were also asked to submit an estimate of the amount of school time they would need to continue with their work. Scheduling of work time for the group was arranged at this meeting and plans were made for subsequent progress reports to the teacher. The children in this class were involved less frequently but in greater depth than those in the third-grade classroom.

Bulletin Boards and Exhibits. After having taught first grade for several years, a teacher moved to the fifth-grade level. In making plans for the first few days of school in September, she decided to plan activities which would permit her to observe how fifth graders in general and the individuals in her class in particular tackled various kinds of problems. One of the activities she planned was to have the class work in six small discussion groups to plan, design, and execute a bulletin board and exhibit.

Across the back of the classroom was a large pegboard bulletin board divided into six four-foot by six-foot panels. At the top of each of these sections the teacher centered a title. The titles were the names of school subjects—Math, Reading, English, Social Studies, Science, and Writing and Spelling. When the children came into the room on the first day of school these bulletin boards were completely blank except for the titles. They were asked to sign up sometime during the day to work on one of the bulletin boards. The sign-up sheets were placed on the counter beneath each section.

On the second day, the teacher explained the task to the whole class. The six groups were to meet and discuss how they would go about making the bulletin board which could be made to include three-dimensional exhibits by using various fixtures in the pegboard. A drawing or mock-up of the group's design was to be submitted to the teacher for approval before actual work on the display was begun. During the discussion periods and subsequent work periods, the teacher was able to observe many styles of working, many kinds of social characteristics, and many ways of approaching a task. She also gained insights into what some children knew, or thought they knew, about the various subjects. The activity served to start the habit and establish the ground rules for pupil-designed-and-made bulletin boards which continued throughout the year.

Programs or Plays. Several fourth-grade youngsters wanted to do something for a student teacher who was soon to leave their class room to go to another assignment. Their teacher asked them to discuss possibilities and report their ideas to her. They ultimately decided they would like to organize a kind of variety show to be presented on the student teacher's last day. This met with the teacher's approval and they planned in greater detail. Several discussions were necessary during the preparations. Each child in the classroom was invited to participate in the performance if he desired. Arrangements were made to borrow a piano from a kindergarten room and to hide other instruments in a nearby classroom until they were needed. A group of youngsters not taking part in the program volunteered to keep the student teacher involved in a mural project in the cafeteria while the performers had an opportunity to rehearse the program on the day before the big event.

The program which resulted amazed even the classroom teacher who was aware of many of the plans. Several piano solos were well spaced throughout the program. These ranged from "Chop Sticks" by an "up-and-coming folk artist" to a medley of classical selections by a "concert pianist." Several solos and duets were played on other instruments. Two magnificent dance numbers were performed by a ten-year-old semiprofessional. Poetry readings and a slapstick pantomime rounded out the program. Children not taking part in the program had made farewell cards and these were presented to the student teacher in a little ceremony. The event was totally the children's, from the conception of the idea to the "last curtain," and they were justifiably proud of it.

Book Talks

Many teachers have wondered if an individualized reading program doesn't make group discussion of stories rather difficult. "How can several children talk about the story if they aren't all reading the same story?" they ask. This presents no problem at all to the children. They simply tell about whatever story they are reading. The "audience" is interested in listening to someone talk about a new or different story.

The children in one second-grade class had small group discussions about books they were reading. They called these discussions "Book Talks," and they looked forward eagerly to each Book Talk day. During these discussions each child had a turn to talk about one of the stories he had read since the last Book Talk. If another had read the story also, he might add to the discussion. Children who had read similar stories, commented on these. Near the end of the discussion time the teacher asked the members of the group to see if they could find some ways in which the stories discussed today were like each other and some ways in which they were different from each other. These similarities and differences were then reported to the whole class. Comments such as, "Our stories were all funny ones," or "We all read about animals but sometimes the animals talked like people and sometimes they didn't," or "Johnny and Steve read *real* stories but the rest of us read make-believe ones," were common.

This type of activity, while less structured than a teacher-centered reading group question and answer period, is more truly a discussion, and is accompanied by far less boredom and fidgeting. Where a teacher wants to check comprehension, by asking questions about a story, he can do it more effectively and efficiently in an individual conference.

Visiting Time

This is probably one of the most needed and least provided for talking experiences in our schools. Children need time to just visit—to talk with friends and classmates about the things that are important to them. These important things may be last night's television programs, how many times Joanne skipped rope without missing, Phil's new model car, the dog across the street that ate part of Anne's lunch this morning, or what the world looked like from the airplane when Ted went to New York last weekend. Informal discussions such as this are an important part of growing up for youngsters. They provide opportunities for developing social awareness, for finding out that all people have strengths *and* weaknesses, for learning that they have many mutual interests and mutual concerns, and for learning the "rules" of social interaction.

Teachers have found that in addition to the value it has for children, scheduling visiting times has many side advantages for the classroom environment. It provides a built-in 15- or 20-minute change-of-pace activity morning and afternoon. Children return to other activities refreshed. Some of the strains of classroom control tend to be relieved with this practice. When children know they are going to have time to visit with friends legally, they don't seem to feel the need to do so at unauthorized times. Visiting time also gives the teacher one more opportunity to find out more about the various needs and interests of the children. Occasionally something that is overheard during visiting time can be recalled and brought into a learning situation. Ted's airplane trip, for example, could fit into a lesson about maps, land forms, transportation, or cities. Or it could serve as a jumping-off place for a variety of art experiences. These results of visiting time are only extras, of course. The real value of such informal discussion time is found in the relaxed social opportunities it provides for youngsters.

SUMMARY

Children need plenty of opportunity to talk in school. Some of the speaking and discussing activities will be highly structured and have specific learning goals. Others will be informal in varying degrees and somewhat open-ended in nature. A good program will have a balance of both structured and unstructured discussion opportunities. Such a program will also have a balance between whole-class and small-group discussion or reporting. Many educational objectives can be served through group discussions. A variety of skills, including those of oral communication and social cooperation, can be enhanced. Changes in understandings and attitudes can sometimes be accomplished through group discussions. Participation in discussion activities can vary with individual needs and interests. The teacher's role involves designing the basic discussion program, modifying it for individual needs, and supporting (but not leading) the actual discussions. Examples of structured discussion activities for skill development, concept formation, and in group dynamics, problem-solving and value clarification have been given. Suggestions have also been included for a variety of unstructured discussion activities.

NINE

Asking Questions:
A Closer Look

Today's teacher may choose from an increasingly large variety of educational tools and paraphernalia. Each year sees the introduction of new audio-visual materials, kits, multilevel texts, software and hardware of all kinds. It would be wise to remember that the teaching question is still the most potentially effective and inexpensive teaching tool available.

As schooling became more formalized, increased emphasis was placed upon standardized evaluations of one sort or another. The question, which had characterized the Socratic method, lost much of its teaching power and was transformed into a testing device. While the need to test still retains importance for classroom teachers, a distinction must be made between the characteristics of teaching questions and testing questions.

TEACHING QUESTIONS	TESTING QUESTIONS
1. Are used throughout a learning sequence to advance learning.	1. Are used at the end of a learning sequence to measure learning.
2. Lead the learner to discover principles which have broad possible applications.	2. Seek to determine which principles or "facts" a student has mastered.
3. Can be adapted to individual need and readiness.	3. Are generally the same for all students.

4. Help the teacher to capitalize on the analysis of many errors made to determine what areas of misconception must be clarified for the learner.

5. Are diagnostic.

6. Are not graded or marked formally.

7. Are invaluable in programs which seek to serve individual differences.

8. Have no threat connotations to the learner, i.e. fear of failure, the embarrassment of being wrong, etc.

4. Help test givers to total the number of errors in order to determine a score or grade.

5. Are evaluative.

6. Are graded and marked formally.

7. Have value in programs which seek to serve individual differences only when the results of testing are analyzed to determine individual need, or when the testing schedule is determined by each individual's readiness to be tested for mastery.

8. Have a high degree of threat connotation to the learner.

CLASSIFYING QUESTIONS

All questions require some degree of mental gymnastics. Questions can be classified into levels of difficulty by analyzing the thinking level which is required to answer them.

Level I.   The Recognition Question

Sample: Find and point to the sentence which tells what mother made.

Thinking Required: The teacher assumes that the reading vocabulary is known; the learner must recognize when he has found the answer. The directive to point to the answer requires no verbalization and is effective with learners who have trouble verbalizing answers.

Sample: Tell me the title of today's story.

Thinking Required: The teacher assumes that the word

title is understood. The learner must apply his understanding by recognizing when he encounters an example of the term. His answer must be given verbally, which requires more skill and involvement than a directive to point.

Sample: List the kinds of food which you see pictured here.

Thinking Required: Again the vocabulary is assumed. The learner must recognize examples of a class (foods). The answer must be written and requires a more difficult level of skills mastery than either of the previous examples.

Level II. The Recall Question

Sample: How is the hero in today's story like the hero in yesterday's story?

Thinking Required: The teacher assumes that the learner recognized the heroic qualities of the character in yesterday's story, that he remembers these qualities and can recall this information, and identify the characteristics of the hero read about today.

Sample: Did this story (date given) take place before or after the Civil War?

Thinking Required: The teacher assumes that the learner can recall the date of the Civil War. The learner must have recognized the date of the story and be able to recall and compare the two dates.

Level III. The Inference Question

Sample: Do you think this story took place before or after the invention of the cotton gin? (No date given.)

Thinking Required: The learner must recall understandings of the effect of the cotton gin on human endeavor and recall the nature of human endeavor described in the story. Next he must mentally contrast his two sets of recall and infer an answer.

Sample: Do you think the women in this picture own as many electrical appliances as women in our town?

Thinking Required: The learner must recall all of the things he knows about electrical appliances, standards of living, and the outward manifestations of labor-saving devices. His answer will be an educated guess, something he infers by contrasting sets of knowledge. Inference questions require the learner to utilize more than one set of unaer-standings in hypothesizing possible solutions.

Level IV.   Justification Question

Sample: Why do you feel that this story was written before the invention of the cotton gin?

Thinking Required: The learner must validate his answer based on the previous inference. He must clarify his thinking process in order to justify his answer.

Sample: How did you determine that the women pictured here own as many appliances as a woman living in our town?

Thinking Required: The learner must tell all of the characteristics which he considers evidence of appliance ownership which he has recognized in the picture. He justifies his answer by giving substantiating proof for his original inference.

Most of the questions asked in pupil workbooks, texts, and teachers manuals are recall and recognition questions. Some series (i.e. *Man in Action,* Prentice-Hall; *Math Workshop,* Encyclopaedia Britannica; SRA Reading Laboratory® series *Reading for Understanding,* Holt, Rinehart & Winston; *Reading and Thinking Skills,* The Continental Press, Inc.) have been designed to build thinking abilities and to develop more complex comprehensions, skills and understandings, but for most teachers the scarcity of appropriate commercial material will require the formulation of original question sequences to supplement existing materials.

Figure 9-1 shows an example of such a question sequence based on study of a picture.

Differentiating Instruction Through Levels of Question Difficulty

Children differ in the development of their thinking abilities. The story in Figure 9-2 was written by an intermediate teacher for a group of children who were relatively homogeneous in reading level but differed in their comprehension or thinking skills

1. What work do you see being done?
2. How is this street like any street you might find in the downtown area of our city? List all the similarities.
3. List all the ways this street differs from some of our downtown streets.
4. Are things being sold on this street? How do you know?
5. Would you expect the people to be very healthy? Why did you answer this way?
6. Did these people have automobiles and trucks to transport things? What clues are in the picture to prove your answer?
7. Can you think of some reasons why these people lived so close to one another?
   (Think about question six again.)

Figure 9–1 *

*Drawing from *History of Early People*, Rand McNally & Company, 1961. Reproduced with permission of the publisher.

level. The questions which were used with this story were assigned to specific children according to the difficulty of the questions. Those in Set I were relatively simple, requiring the learner to function at the recognition level. Questions in Sets II and III became somewhat more involved and complex.

Reading Detectives
Figure 9–2

The water lapped gently against the dock. Out on the lake a sailboat stood listlessly, moving hardly at all. Another boat floated lazily between the sailboat and the shore where the dock was. Two figures were seated in it with their backs to the sailboat. Long, thin poles extended from their hands out over the water. It was late in the afternoon and the figures cast a shadow before them that almost reached the dock. Finally the two men gave up their fruitless efforts, pulled up the anchor and rowed toward the dock. Fastening the boat to the end of the dock, they picked up their poles and the oars and climbed out. The boat, empty except for the anchor, bobbed up and down, rubbing gently against the dock.

Set I

1. How many people were in the rowboat?
2. What other kind of boat was on the lake?
3. What time of day was it?

Set II

1. Which boat was farthest from the dock?
2. Did the men succeed at what they were doing?
3. What things were in the boat as the men rowed toward the dock?

Set III

1. Was it calm or rough on the water? How do you know?
2. Was the dock on the north, east, south or west shore of the lake? How do you know?
3. Draw a picture showing what you would have seen if you had been on the sailboat while the men were still on the lake.

INDUCTIVE AND DEDUCTIVE LEARNING

Although no learning process is totally inductive or deductive, there are basic differences between these processes. Deductive methods begin with an explanation of the big idea or concept generalization and utilize supportive facts to demonstrate the truth and applicability of the generalization. An inductive method presents the learner with various examples of a given concept and encourages the learner to generalize.

A discovery approach is essentially an inductive approach. The learner is led through a series of teacher- or self-initiated questions to perceive and understand examples of a concept. When a sufficient number of examples has been studied, the learner is encouraged to generalize about the concept, based on that individual learner's understanding of the relationships between the examples studied.

Imagine that you wanted to utilize an inductive discovery approach in teaching phonetic rules to your class. You might list a number of three letter words which have a short vowel sound.

cap
man
pan
men
tap
rip
rot
cut

Next you would work back through a series of questions which would guide the learner to see the relationship between the words.

How many letters does each word have?

Are there any other ways in which these words are alike?

How many vowels are there in each word?

Do you hear a long vowel or a short vowel in cap? (Or man, pan, etc.)

Who can make a reading rule that would be true for each of these words?

Once you have helped the group to generalize about vowel sounds in short words, you could encourage them to test their generalization with other words.

Children who are given ample experience in seeking out principles and generalizations are apt to understand the generalizations better and to apply them more often than they would have if they had been simply told all of the rules by their teacher.

The effective teacher will have to decide when to use a deductive approach and when to use an inductive approach. Giving children a set of rules or generalizations will often demand the least amount of training time, and will often be the most efficient way to guide children. Less efficient in terms of time, but often more effective because of the high degree of pupil involvement, a discovery approach can best serve the learner in determining the structure of knowledge and values.

CONSTRUCTING TESTS TO DIAGNOSE LEARNING NEEDS

How often do we test children, score the results and record a mark, without taking the time to determine just what went wrong when an error was made?

Standardized achievement tests are usually handled in this way. Knowing that a given child received a certain score does not tell us exactly what a child has mastered nor does it pinpoint areas of specific disability. Another drawback to approaching testing in the "score and record a grade" fashion is the lack of communication to the learner of just what it is that he must now learn. Feedback to the learner should be a part of our educational testing program.

The following multiple choice questions are designed to tell us something about the learner.

1. 3^2 is equal to

   a) 6 (the exponent was misinterpreted as 2 times 3)

   b) 9 (the exponent is correctly interpreted)

   c) 5 (the exponent was misinterpreted as 3 plus 2)

2. Each night Mary liked to wish on a

   a) start (ending error)
   b) rats (orientation error)
   c) stor (middle error)
   d) star

Commercial diagnostic tests are frequently constructed in this way. Other diagnostic tests depend upon the sequence of questions to determine the point along a continuum at which learning breaks down.

LISTENING TO CHILDREN'S QUESTIONS AND ANSWERS

Diagnostic teaching-learning techniques often utilize information gleaned in informal, nontesting situations. The most frequently overlooked technique is simply listening to children and hearing what they say.

Statements Teachers Should Question

Children are often communicating concern and confusion about the process of learning when they speak about themselves.

When a child says this:	*It might mean this*:
I DON'T GET IT.	I have learned that there is a right and a wrong way to do everything. Rather than be wrong again, I'll place the responsibility for understanding outside myself.
I HATE MATH.	I don't understand the under lying principles of this unimportant and unreal science.
I REALLY LIKE SCIENCE.	For some unknown reason I click here. I'm rewarded with good grades and I feel good about myself.

I'M STUPID.	I've given up trying. I don't much like myself and I don't know why.
I'M SMART.	I do what I'm supposed to. I get good marks and my parents are proud of me. Getting ahead is going to be easy for me. I'll just continue to follow directions.
I'M NOT STUPID.	I am trying; I spent a lot of time figuring things out. I'm confused and don't know why my answer is often wrong.
MY DAD WILL KILL ME IF I FLUNK.	I see little real purpose for school. I don't understand half of what's going on. School is important to my father. My father accepts grades as evidence of my worth.
I GET A DOLLAR FOR EVERY A.	I carry a lot of responsibility for my family's worth. If I do well it means that they are successful parents.
DOES THIS TEST COUNT?	I take no responsibility for my own time. Unless I am constantly directed I waste my time. The only worthwhile learning activities are teacher-directed.
WHY WAS MY MARK SO LOW ON MY REPORT CARD?	I know that grades are determined by a kind of secret formula. I don't know what your teaching objectives were. I've begun to be a little bit self-diagnostic and I thought I'd figured out what you wanted.
DID WE GO OVER THIS IN CLASS?	I have no more responsibility than to parrot back what you say.

WHEN ARE WE GOING TO GET TO STUDY JAPAN?	I have a lot of interest in and knowledge about Japan. I'm sure to do well when we study it
WHO IS YOUR FAVORITE STUDENT?	I'm trying to figure out who I should try to be like. You don't seem to like me.
WHO IS YOUR FAVORITE POET?	I've decided I want to be like you.
DID YOU READ *Stuart Little?*	I value the ideas we share when we talk over something.

Some Questions to Expect

As you move toward a differentiated and more individualized program, be prepared to answer new types of child-initiated questions.

Do we have to . . . ? As children are encouraged to develop their own interests and talents, this question will come up. Perhaps it is only one child who doesn't want to do math today, or a group who have become so involved with a particular project that they wish to continue. Because you as teacher are the leader of the group, you will have to think carefully about how you will answer this type of question. As a guideline, it is always easier to retain your leadership than to regain it. There will frequently be times when as leader you must say "you will do it because I said you should." A scheduled conference with an individual or group who dissent can be eye-opening and constructive, while hasty decisions to scrap an agreed-upon schedule can be distructive.

MY answer is different from the key. Is it wrong? Frequently a child's answer will be phrased in an equivalent way. At other times the individual's frame of reference has shaded the meaning of the question or its answer. The teacher must review the student's thinking in order to help him understand why his answer is equally correct or to clarify what if anything was wrong in his thinking.

Questioning answer keys is one sign that children are becoming self-evaluative, and it is always possible that the keys themselves are wrong.

ANOTHER LOOK

Questions may well prove to be the most important tool, and the one you use most often as you move to differentiate instruction. In planning learning sequences, utilize questions at all levels of thinking ability in order to guide children to effectively learn from their environment and experiences.

Construct tests which pinpoint specific ability and disability. Review the test results with each child. Help each learner to see the progress that he has made and to set a realistic plan for accomplishing the next goal.

Learn to question the surface communications and interactions that constitute classroom living. Only when we really know each student as a unique and special individual can we hope to begin to plan an appropriate course of individualized instruction.

TEN

Guided
Listening Activities

The selection and structure of guided listening experiences can serve a variety of purposes in the classroom. Perhaps the most obvious is that of providing opportunities to strengthen and refine the skills of listening as a concomitant of communication. Other kinds of guided listening activities can be utilized to assist in your program of skill development in subject areas such as reading and mathematics. A third function is that of serving as a vehicle for structuring independent learning experiences. The purpose or objective for a specific listening activity might become an important factor in the selection of the method of presentation to be used. Where independent learning opportunities are being provided, disc or tape recordings could be very appropriate. Where skill development is involved, live presentation of the listening experience would be as satisfactory as recordings, though more demanding of your classroom time. Live presentations give the added advantage of interaction and feedback between students and teacher.

Individualizing a program of listening activities involves careful selection and structuring of the listening experience according to the various needs, abilities, and interests in a given classroom. Providing 30 unique listening activities for 30 children would, of course, be impractical if not impossible and would be of doubtful value. Groups of up to six or eight pupils can often benefit from the same listening exercise and are a convenient size for working with headsets at a listening center. Planning a listening experience for a small group requires consideration of many factors regarding the children in the group. How sophisticated is their listening vocabulary? How well and for how long can they work as a group without direct supervision? How complex a task can they comfortably handle? What kinds of listening opportunities do they need?

The suggestions and experiences that follow were planned for a variety of vocabulary levels and study habits. They vary in duration and complexity as well as in the purposes for which they have been designed. An attempt has been made to draw from many subject areas and grade levels in an effort to provide a wide sampling of guided listening activities to challenge your thinking.

LISTENING AS A COMPONENT OF COMMUNICATION

Listening is one aspect of communication which is often overlooked or taken for granted in our educational programs. The activities discussed in this section have the development of listening skills as their primary objective. This objective has, in turn, been broken down into more specific targets of listening for a given purpose—to hear details, to recognize a mood, or for critical analysis.

Listening for Details

This activity was designed for use with a tape recorder to help a group of primary pupils in listening carefully to hear details. A similar activity could be used with older children simply by making it slightly more sophisticated.

A collection of objects was placed on a table. Included in the collection were a white china bowl, a white plastic bottle cap, a rubber bottle "cork," a white plastic drinking glass, a round silver bell (such as a teacher might have on his desk), a ball bearing, and a white golf ball. Each object was numbered. The children, seated around the table, listened to the tape with earphones. They were instructed to study the objects on the table as they listened. They would hear the objects described one at a time.

When each description was completed, they were to write on their papers the number of the object just described. The descriptions were given in such a way that the first clue would describe several of the objects. Each successive clue narrowed down the possibilities until a single item had been identified. Part of the taped monologue included the following clues.

> The first object you are to find is sort of roundish but is not shaped like a ball. (*This described all items except the golf ball and the ball bearing.*)
> It would most likely be found in the kitchen. (*This eliminated the bell.*)
> It is white. (*This narrowed the possibilities to the bowl, the glass, and the plastic bottle cap.*)
> You would probably use it to put something in. (*This eliminated the bottle cap.*)
> This object is bigger around than it is tall. What is it? (*pause*) Did you write number three for the bowl? I was describing the white bowl. Let's try another one.
> The second object is fairly small.
> It is a useful object.
> You would probably find it in the kitchen
> It is made of rubber. What is it?

Timing of the clues is important in this type of activity. The child must have ample opportunity to eliminate objects and identify all remaining possibilities and yet he must not have enough time to forget other clues that have already been given. A little practice in preparing this type of activity will enable the teacher to pace the clues effectively.

In the activity described above, physical objects were used and the children responded simply by writing the number of the object. Pictures could also be used very effectively. Older children would be able to respond by writing the name of the object. They could also be confronted with a greater number of objects from which to choose and could be given clues of a more subtle nature.

Recognizing Mood

A fifth-grade teacher prepared a series of oral reading presentations. Each presentation consisted of about ten short poems or selections from stories or essays each of which described or expressed a particular mood. The children were asked to listen to each selection and to react to it in terms of what kind of mood it expressed. No discussion was permitted at this time. The purpose in withholding discussion was to give each child complete freedom in identifying the mood of the selection. By demanding silent written responses, prompting by the more spontaneous and verbal children was prevented.

After all the selections had been read and all the reactions recorded, a discussion was held. The children compared their reactions and frequently asked to have a selection reread to support a point. No attempt was made to select the one *right* answer for any selection. Instead the children were encouraged to react naturally to the mood of the reading and were permitted to explain why the selection made them feel happy, frightened, excited, uncomfortable, gloomy, etc. A climate of acceptance pervaded the discussion, and the teacher commented frequently on how interesting it was to notice that many times the children had reacted differently to the same reading.

Critical Analysis

We often hear teachers and parents lament that children believe everything they hear. In today's world of television and radio it is indeed vitally important to give children opportunities to critically analyze things they are hearing. One way of doing this is to plan a series of discussions based on short listening experiences.

Commercials. Bring a radio or television set into the classroom. Arrange to have a group of children listen to a few commercials. Quite often three or four commercials will be given one after another at the hour or half-hour break in broadcasting. This listening experience should be followed immediately with a teacher-guided discussion of what was heard. Not all of the com mercials need to be analyzed in the discussion; one or two might serve just as well. Depending upon the content of the commercial such questions as the following might be posed to stimulate the discussion.

How much of the commercial was devoted to giving facts; how much to giving opinions?

What were some of the words used to describe the product?

What technique was used to make you want to buy the product?

Did the advertisement try to make competitive brands look inferior? How?

If a statement is used such as, "There is no product better than ours," ask if this means the product being advertised is, therefore, better than all others or does it mean that it is equal to others?

What claims are made for the product and how are these claims substantiated? Are there any loopholes in their proof?

What devices are used to illustrate what happens (inside the body, for example) when the product is used? Is the device really representative of the thing being illustrated?

Does the advertisement use fancy names or symbols for ingredients in the product to make them sound especially effective or powerful?

What slogans, songs, or other techniques are used to help you remember the name of the product?

Statistics. When the television or radio commercial being heard includes the use of statistics, some children might benefit from a follow-up activity based on obtaining statistical data. Select a controversial issue such as some current fad in fashions or hair styles to serve as the focus for the activity. Have half of the group attempt to obtain statistics which prove that *three out of four people interviewed are in favor of* the issue in question. The other half of the group should attempt to obtain statistics showing that *three out of four people interviewed are opposed to* the issue.

Direct both groups to begin by drawing up a list of names of at least 20 specific people with whom interviews are likely to result in the obtaining of desired opinions. The children should then conduct the survey and follow this by an analysis of the data. If their data does not indicate exactly *three out of four* persons giving the desired response, have the group consider ways in which the actual data can be used to support their position in the controversy. The members of each group could then prepare a commercial to sell their idea. Visuals, demonstrations, slogans, music—any appropriate advertising device—could be utilized. These commercials could be presented live or on tape to other children in the class. The presentations could be followed by a discussion of how the substantiating statistics had been obtained; who had been interviewed and why they had been selected to be interviewed.

LISTENING EXPERIENCES IN SKILL AREAS

The suggestions and experiences in the previous section of this chapter were designed for the development of skills of listening. Those presented in this section use the skills of listening to assist in the development of other kinds of skills. Here are examples of how guided listening activities can help provide opportunities for developing readiness in reading and math, for adding variety to drill, and for giving practice in and extending study skills.

Reading

Reading, being an academic skill area comprised of many sub-skills, lends itself readily to the use of listening activities. Activities involving visual discrimination, vocabulary development, comprehension, word attack skills, and reference skills can all be presented as guided listening experiences using live or tape recorded presentations. Some commercially available disc and tape recordings are suitable for this type of activity where only brief oral instructions are required to get the task under way. Two specific examples of taped lessons in reading are given below. The first shows several ways of using a single material at various times with a group of children, any of which could be used at other times with other groups. The second is an example of an activity which was designed for a specific purpose for a specific group of children and was not reused with other groups.

Using Workbooks. Many beginning reading workbooks have pages which can be used for activities in addition to the ones suggested in the teachers' guide. One such page consisting of five rows of pictures with four pictures in each row was used for two widely different kinds of listening activities: an exercise in initial consonant sounds and one in making inferences.

The taped instructions for the first activity went like this.

> Turn in your workbook to page six. (*pause*) Put your marker on the page and move it down so you can see the first row of pictures. (*pause*) There are four pictures in this row. You should see a mailman, a sailboat, a seven, and a mouse.
>
> Now I am going to say a word. Listen carefully to the sound at the beginning of the word. Then look at the pictures in the first row in your workbook. Find two things whose names begin with the same sound. Put an "X" on those pictures. Ready? Here is the word ... mother ... mother. Put an "X" on the two things that begin with the same sound as *mother.* (*pause*) You should have put an "X" on mailman and mouse because those words begin like mother.
>
> Move your marker down so you can see the second row of pictures. Listen to the word I am going to say and find two things that have the same beginning sound. Ready? The word is something ... something. ...

The tape continues in this manner, correcting each row as soon as the children have had time to do the work for that row. At another time the children use the same page with a different tape for an exercise in making inferences, an excerpt of which follows.

> Move your marker down so you can see the next row of pictures. (*The pictures show some money, a safety pin, a pair of scissors, and a map.*)
>
> Mother went to the table to get something. She needed something sharp. She wanted to cut some cloth with it. Put a ring around the thing that mother probably picked up. (*pause*) Did you put a ring around the scissors? Mother would probably have used the scissors to cut the cloth.
>
> Move your marker down to the next row of pictures. (*Here the children see pictures of a monkey, a man, a seal, and a stamp.*)
>
> Tommy saw some interesting things at the zoo. Some of the animals he saw were good climbers and some were good swimmers. Put a ring around a good climber that Tommy might have seen at the zoo.

The rest of this activity continues in the same manner. The same page in this workbook could also have been used for other exercises in:

> *following directions*—Find the picture of the man; color his hair brown. Find the picture of the mouse; draw a line over his head.
>
> *vocabulary development*—Look at the first row of pictures. Now find the word written on the board which names one of the pictures. Write the word under the correct picture.

Controlled Vocabulary Stories. A fourth-grade teacher was working with a group of children having severe reading difficulties. Some of the children had not yet mastered many pre-primer vocabulary words. The activity described here was designed for six children ranging in age from nine to eleven, all of whom needed to work at beginning reading levels.

The teacher began by giving individual word recognition inventories to each child, identifying all pre-primer and primer words the child was able to read. She then analyzed the inventory data to find a list of words which none of the children knew (or in some cases, words which five of the six children did not know) and a list of words which all of them knew. She then created a series of stories using the known words. Names of children in the group were also used. One new word was introduced on each page. The word was written at the top of the page and used in as many sentences as possible on that page. Each sentence occupied one line of the page. The word was then used frequently on succeeding pages together with the other new words. (See Figure 10-1.)

These stories were duplicated and assembled into booklets with a copy of each booklet for each child.

The teacher then prepared a tape on which she read each story, one sentence at a time, with a long pause between each one. A signal was given for turning pages, the new word at the top of the next page was read, and the story continued. When the children listened to the story with the earphones they had a copy of the booklet with them. The teacher gave oral directions on how to proceed before she turned on the tape recorder. The first time the children heard a story, they listened to each sentence as it was

Something for Nancy

here

Mrs. Green said, "Nancy, come here!"
Nancy said, "Here I am, Mother."
"Something is here for you," said Mrs. Green
"Uncle Jack's surprise is here!"
"What is it?" said Nancy.
"What is in the box?"
"Here it is," said Mrs. Green.
"Look and see what it is."

have

"Oh, good! I have a surprise!"
"I have a surprise box," said Nancy.
"Here, Mother. I will look in it."
Mrs. Green said, "What do you have in the box?"
"I have a funny big kitten!"
"May I see your kitten?" said Mrs. Green.
"Yes, you may have it. Here it is."
"What will you do with the kitten?"
"I have a bed for it," said Nancy.
"I will put it here in the bed."

Controlled Vocabulary Stories
Figure 10–1

read on the tape. Then they repeated the sentence aloud softly
during the pause that followed. The second time they listened
to the story, they read each sentence aloud softly during the pause
that came *before* it and then listened as the sentence was read on
the tape. This enabled them to check themselves and to hear the
correct pronunciation of any word which might still trouble them.

The same stories were used for reading aloud to each other in
pairs and for occasional group oral reading and discussion with
the teacher. The children also drew pictures (on the back of the
preceding page of the booklet), to illustrate some event on each

page of the story requiring comprehension of that section of the story.

Admittedly this activity required a great deal of preparation time on the part of the teacher. She felt that the needs of the children warranted the extra time and effort, and she felt amply rewarded by their enthusiasm and by the increase in their reading vocabularies during this time.

Mathematics

Teachers planning for instruction in mathematics are confronted with two persistent problems which challenge the ingenuity of even the most creative. One of these is the problem of providing sufficient opportunities for manipulating concrete objects prior to the introduction of the symbolic representation of some mathematical concept or operation. For example, a child should have many chances to use real things—blocks, pebbles, buttons, etc.—to find that 21 objects, when rearranged into groups of three, will provide seven groups, before he is asked to represent this symbolically by writing

$$21 \div 3 = 7$$

or

$$3\overline{)21.}^{\,7.}$$

The second problem is that of finding ways to vary the diet of drill and practice. Guided listening activities offer new possibilities for approaching these problems.

Directing Concrete Experiences. A teacher wishing to give manipulative experiences with fractional parts of groups planned this activity for a group of primary children before introducing them to written exercises such as these.

$$\tfrac{1}{3} \text{ of } 15 = \square$$

$$\square = \tfrac{1}{4} \text{ of } 12$$

Each child in the group was given a box of small cubical counting blocks and a sheet of standard white typing paper. They were seated at the listening center where a tape recording provided oral instructions directing them to:

> Fold the paper into two sections.
> Put eight blocks on the left side of the paper.
> Now move one out of every four of these to the right side of the paper.
> How many blocks did you move to the right side? You should have moved two.
> Clear the paper and start again.
> This time put twelve blocks on the left side of the paper.
> Move one out of every three of these to the right side of the paper....

A variation on these instructions directed the students to:

> Put nine blocks on the sheet of paper.
> Arrange these into three groups so that each group has the same number of blocks.
> How many blocks are in each group...?

Still later, the youngsters were given a ditto sheet with pictures of groups of objects and were told to:

> Look at the picture of the group of dogs.
> How many dogs are in the group? (*pause*)
> Did you count six dogs in the group?
> Draw a ring around one-half of the group of dogs.
> One-half of a group of six is how many? (*pause*) Did you say *three*...?

After several sessions such as these the children were ready to begin the written exercises. They were encouraged to draw pictures to help them solve these problems, similar to the way they had worked with the tape recorder. Very little difficulty was encountered and most of the children soon outgrew the need for drawing illustrations to solve the exercises.

Providing Opportunities for Drill and Practice. Often a teacher will find that a few children need more practice than usual in reading and writing large numbers. This two-part activity can be presented live or by means of the tape recorder. The use of the tape recorder gives the child just as much practice as presentation by the teacher, but a teacher-presented activity also provides feedback to the teacher.

The first part of the exercise presents a list of numbers, on a ditto sheet if the tape recorder is used or written on the board, one at a time, if presented by the teacher. A technique like that used with the controlled vocabulary stories described earlier in the chapter is used with these numbers. The first time, the number is read aloud and the children repeat it. The second time through the list, the children read the number orally and then listen as the tape or the teacher says the number while they check to see if they have read it correctly.

In the second part of the exercise, numbers are dictated to the children while they write them down. The correct form for writing each number is given as soon as enough time has elapsed for the number to have been written. The taped dialogue for this part of the exercise might go like this,

> Write this number: six hundred forty-seven thousand, two hundred three... six hundred forty-seven thousand, two hundred three.... Now check your work: six, four, seven, comma, two, zero, three.
> Here is another number for you to write.

If the numbers are being dictated by the teacher, the same format would be used except that the teacher would write the number on the board after the children have had an opportunity to write it. The children in this case would then check their work visually.

Following Directions

Very careful listening and precise following of directions are required for this exercise in map building. Children who are asked to do this activity should have had previous experience in making maps and need to be able to immediately locate north, east, southeast, northwest, etc. on a map.

Each child in the group is given a sheet of paper with an outline of a city drawn on it. The outline is a simple oblong shape. Instructions for building the map are given on the tape recorder, one at a time. The children are told to turn off the recorder after each instruction while they complete that portion of the map. You might like to take a few extra minutes now, as you read the directions that follow, to build one of these maps. It will give you an idea of the thought processes required to do the exercise and will alert you to some of the problems the children might encounter.

1. Put Main Street through the center of the city running east and west. Label it.

2. First Street runs north and south near the east edge of the city. Put it on your map and label it.

3. Third Street runs north and south near the west edge of the city. Put it on your map and label it.

4. Put Second Street where you would expect to see it. Label it.

5. North Avenue is north of Main Street. It starts at Second Street and runs out the east side of the city. Draw it on your map and label it.

6. South Avenue runs between First Street and Third Street. Put it on the side of Main Street where you think its name shows it would go. Label it.

7. Put a small lake near the northeast corner of Third Street and Main Street.

8. Be careful now! A river goes from the lake, flows northeast, passes under Second Street and First Street, and runs out the northeast corner of the city. Show the river on your map.

9. Don't forget to put bridges where they will be needed.

10. Now show a railroad. The railroad comes into the northwest corner of the city. It crosses Main Street and goes out the south edge of the city.

11. Use symbols to show the locations of some of the buildings which might be in this city.

12. Make a key or legend for your map.

STRUCTURING LISTENING ACTIVITIES FOR INDEPENDENT LEARNING

The teacher attempting to individualize instruction finds it increasingly important to structure activities which enable children to proceed independently with learning on many fronts. We know, for example, that a given social studies concept or generalization can be taught with a variety of content areas or units. The notion that "many people have made contributions which have benefited our country" can be approached through a study of colonial leaders, inventors, scientists, the Civil War, Jane Addams, American artists and architects, or a great variety of other topics. While the teacher may have as a single objective for all his pupils the study of some specific examples, he can individualize the study by varying the routes through which the children will approach this notion. Topics can be selected according to interest. Children could work alone, in pairs, or in small groups. The selection of materials would be guided by the child's topic, his reading level and study habits, and by the availability of a variety of kinds of materials. Commercial disc recordings of dramatizations of events in American history could be used for some of the children. The way in which such records might be used would vary with the children using them.

Check Lists

Some children seem to need a great deal of help in focusing attention on the task at hand. When the task is listening to a record, a check list could prove helpful.

A small group of children had decided to use *Pioneers* as their topic in the study described above. Several records including one on the story of Lewis and Clark were obtained for them to use. The teacher prepared a list of words, names, and phrases that were used in the recorded story. She listed these in the order in which they would be heard as the story unfolded. (See Figure 10-2.)

The children were asked to put a check mark before each word or phrase when it was heard for the first time in the story. This particular group of children found it necessary to listen to the record a second time before the task was mastered. After the

Listening Check List for "Lewis and Clark" Record

Check off these words and phrases as you hear them on the record.

____James Madison	____fancy bracelets
____President Jefferson	____May 13, 1804
____15 million dollars	____grizzled, reddish brown
____a year, even longer	____free election
____Mr. Merriweather Lewis	____Sacagawea, the birdwoman
____Capt. William Clark	____by late April or early May
____fort of St. Louis	____horses for our expedition
____1804	____320 acres of fine land

Figure 10–2

listening part of the activity was over, the children were asked to use the check list as a guide for a discussion of the story. They were to read each word or phrase and talk about how it fit in the story.

Listening Guides

Two other children were studying Benjamin Franklin. In addition to biographies from the library, a recorded biographical sketch was provided for these boys to use. A listening guide was prepared to help them in finding pertinent information from the record. This guide consisted of a list of questions which they read before listening to the story. (See Figure 10-3.)

As they listened to the record, each boy jotted down notes which would help him remember the answer to the question. Later they compared notes to see if they agreed on the answers. Where disagreements existed, portions of the record were played again to help clarify the issue. It was not considered necessary for them to write formal responses to the questions. The listening guide was meant to assist them in listening and was not designed to serve as a written check on their learnings.

Listening Guide for "Benjamin Franklin" Record

Read all these questions aloud with your partner. Listen to the record. As you listen, write down a few notes to help you remember the answers to the questions. After the record is over, discuss the answers with your partner. Use your notes to help you.

1. Where was Ben Franklin going on the ship *Reprisal*? Why was he going?
2. What danger was the ship in on its voyage?
3. What and where was Ben Franklin's first job?
4. Where did he go from there?
5. What name did Ben Franklin give to the books he wrote and published?
6. When he started his own newspaper, what purpose did he use it for?
7. Were all of Ben Franklin's experiments with electricity successful?
8. What were some of Ben Franklin's inventions?
9. Why did the Pennsylvania Assembly send him to England in 1757?
10. What was he able to obtain from France?
11. What two important documents did Ben Franklin help to write?
12. Try to remember all the things he did which helped other Americans.

Figure 10–3

SUMMARY

Three major types of guided listening activities have been discussed in this chapter. The development of listening skills is valuable as an end in itself. We have examined techniques of providing opportunities to practice listening for details, to recognize moods, and for critical analysis. Listening skills can be used as a means to an end, as when they are used in acquiring academic and study skills. Illustrative activities falling in this category have been drawn from the areas of reading, math, and social studies. Listening activities also serve as one method of providing for independent learning, permitting you to capitalize on the fact that an idea or notion can be taught in several ways and *via* many different topics simultaneously. Check lists and listening guides are useful materials for this purpose.

ELEVEN

Making
Toys and Games
Meaningful

Today's classroom is likely to have an assortment of "educational games." Occasionally these materials are used in a teacher-directed drill lesson. More often they are used as a special incentive or reward to encourage children to finish all their assigned work. When used in the latter way, we create problems for ourselves. The game or toy is such an attractive inducement that some children will rush carelessly through independent assignments. Rarely does the painfully slow or extremely conscientious child have an opportunity to use, enjoy or learn from what are essentially most attractive educational media.

Just what is the educational value of toys and games? Very little if they encourage carelessness in some and frustration in others.

Many educational theorists today suggest that learning is the result of broad experience in manipulating, observing and comparing concrete objects in order to form a basis for abstract and symbolic reasoning. Toys and games can be utilized in planned and sequential learning activities which provide the student with experiences at the concrete-manipulative level. In structuring such a planned sequence, we restore the validity of educational toys and games, not as a reward for completing other assigned work but as valid and valuable play-work assignments.

Many of the ideas which will be discussed in this chapter were developed and first tried with our youngest children. The structuring of learning sequences which allow children to proceed independently poses a unique problem for teachers of children at the prereading or beginning reading levels. When children have not yet developed the skills of reading and writing, most of the materials patterned after those used for independent work at the intermediate level are totally inappropriate. Toys and games had always played an important part in our early primary classes. We analyzed the kinds of play material we had been using and explored our reasons for including this play material in our programs and in our budgets. We soon realized that a more careful planning and structuring of many play experiences could serve valid learning objectives.

Planned play sequences were highly successful with very young children, and the basic idea of structuring learning sequences in this way was expanded to other grade levels. This chapter will discuss "Manipulatives at the Pre-Reading Level" and "Toys and Games Beyond the Primary Grades," although many of the ideas can be modified for all levels.

MANIPULATIVES AT THE PREREADING LEVEL

Beads, peg-boards and many commercial construction toys such as *Rig-a-jig, Playtiles, Parquetry Blocks,* and *Flexigons* can be programmed to develop visual discrimination of size, color and shape, spacial relationships, and eye-hand co-ordination.

Developing Readiness Skills with Beads

Beads are ideal for very young children and a sequence of activities is easily developed.

Level I. Bead patterns are strung for children to duplicate. The attributes of any pattern will be color or shape (of the bead), number (one to one correspondence), and originality. Simple patterns would limit complexity by alternating perhaps only two colors of square beads. The most complex patterns will incorporate many colors and many shapes in random order. At this stage, which might last for several weeks, children work from concrete to concrete in exact replication. See Figure 11-1.

Sample Bead Patterns
Figure 11-1

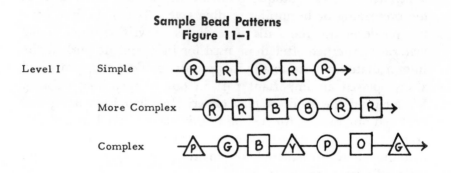

Level I   Simple

            More Complex

            Complex

Level II. This level of the sequence requires the student to string a bead pattern from a drawing of smaller scale. A progression of drawings can be reproduced on ditto to allow a sequence of complexity based on the attribute of shape. Colored felt pens or crayons can then be used to give you a variety of patterns from each of these dittoes. This method of making several patterns from a single ditto master will minimize the preparatory work. At this level children work from a semi-concrete referent to concrete manipulation in preparation for the third level which is essentially a decoding process.

Level III. Work with the children to evolve a code for each type of bead; i.e. Yo stands for yellow oval, Bs for blue square, and Rb for red ball. On separate and numbered cards code each assignment in sequence; i.e. Yo - Yo - Bs - Bb - etc. This level can be made self-correcting simply by stringing a bead pattern to accompany each card. After the children have decoded an assignment they can compare their work with your key.

By leading the child through a progressively more difficult series of playlike tasks, an understanding of the process of encoding and decoding can be developed. As reading is essentially a decoding process, it is essential that a conceptualization of this process be developed before beginning formal reading instruction. Of course, many children do not need this type of experience and are ready to begin formal reading as soon as they enter school. But if we truly differentiate instruction, we will provide ample experience of this type for those children who do require it

Construction Toys

Many of the building toys which are advertised and sold by the larger school supply houses can be adapted for a sequence of play-learning activities. The simplest adaptation is to cut apart the printed illustrated patterns which are usually included with the toy, mount each separately on oak tag, and arrange the patterns in a sequence from simplest to most difficult. Number the patterns according to difficulty and allow the children to work through the sequence. Some of the commercial games which we have found useful for this type of adaptation are *Rig-a-Jig*, *Playtiles*, *Flexigons* and *Colorforms*. If the sequence which is obtained by following the manufacturer's patterns is not appropriate for your learners, additional levels can be developed similar to those used in the bead sequences.

Level I. Make objects with the toys for children to copy. At this level, concrete to concrete, children are developing eye-hand co-ordination, the numerical concept of one-to-one correspondence, and visual discrimination by size, shape and color.

Level II. Supplement the manufacturer's patterns with hand-drawn full-scale drawings of simple patterns. Children frequently need additional practice in inferring a concretion from a picture. Level II gives this type of experience.

Level III. Reduced-scale illustrations such as the ones which accompany the commercial toy would logically be used at this level. The child is called upon to interpret a scale drawing and frequently to infer a hidden side or third dimension.

One resourceful kindergarten teacher took colored slides of many of the designs and patterns which children developed while working with building toys during unstructured free time. These slides were projected into a viewing box to enable an individual or small group to reproduce the design or pattern.

A Multimedia Approach to Manipulatives

Have 4 by 8 foot sheets of hardboard cut into eight two-foot squares. Paint each square green. Next paint on streets in straight lines running parallel with the edges and crossing each other at right angles. Use a different color for each street. An orange street, for example, might run from left to right, while a blue street would run up and down. Since you are going to refer to each street by its color, only one street can be made a given color. Make each of the hardboard maps exactly alike. They may be turned to any of four possible positions which, when coupled with different instructions, will give ample variety.

Prepare a tape of oral directions along these lines: "Find the place where Blue Street crosses Black Street. (pause) Put your finger where Blue Street crosses Black Street. (pause) Move your finger to the space which is up and to the left of that crossing. (pause) Put a block in that space." Timing is important in preparing these tapes. You might find that writing an outline script and recording while you actually work with a small group helps to develop appropriate pacing of oral directions.

Tapes may be prepared at different levels and with more complex directions. As children listen with earphones and construct the village, they are practicing the following oral directions and developing an understanding of fundamental mapping skills.

A variation of this type of oral instruction would be to ask the listener to "Drive the blue car up to the corner of Purple Street and Red Street. (pause) Turn left and drive on Red Street until you reach Black Street. (pause) Leave the blue car there. (pause) Drive the yellow car—etc."

Keys can be made for each tape and stored with the tape. When the children finish listening to the tape they can check their own work against the key, or you can check it with them.

Blocks as Media for Developing Spatial Perceptions

Bags of multishaped blocks can be interestingly programmed into sequences which advance the learner's perception of size and shape. Playing boards are first cut from cardboard or hardboard and marked into rectangles with paint or felt tipped pen. Arrange the blocks, one to each rectangular space, and trace the shape of each block. Remember that there are many faces on each of the blocks. Vary the arrangement of the blocks before you trace them. Some should be placed on end or at angles.

The object of the play-learning session is to select blocks from the set and cover the traced patterns.

More complicated patterns can be developed by determining which blocks will stack one upon the other and tracing the patterns so that this overlapping is inferred. See Figure 11-2.

Sample Bead Patterns for Geometric Blocks
Figure 11–2

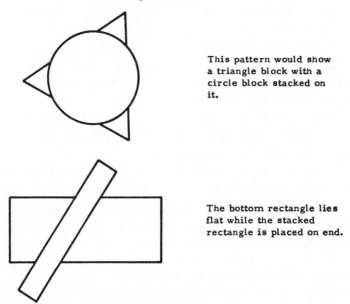

This pattern would show a triangle block with a circle block stacked on it.

The bottom rectangle lies flat while the stacked rectangle is placed on end.

The set of patterns which you develop can be ordered according to difficulty and numbered.

TOYS AND GAMES BEYOND THE PRIMARY LEVEL

Many popular games may be incorporated as is into the educational program. An introduction to probability theory might be developed as an outgrowth of SCRABBLE, tick-tack-toe or bingo.

Practice in finding synonyms might occur in playing PASSWORD. "MIGHT" is the key word. Teacher guidance and planning can optimize the chances that desirable learnings will take place. By studying the type of skills, knowledges and understandings which are necessary to play a given game successfully, you can de velop programs to use that game profitably.

Children should be made aware of the objectives which you hope to attain by using a specific game. If the game is fun and also a good way to drill on math facts, the children should be aware of the learning bonus which they get as they enjoy themselves.

An example of this type of drill activity is Multiples-of-Three Dominoes. Each player draws eight tiles. The first child to turn up a multiple of three starts the play. Turns are taken in a clockwise order. Each player is allowed to add one tile per turn. The resulting total in a line of tiles must be a multiple of three. If the child is going to use the dots in both halves of the tile, he continues the line he is adding to. If he is only going to use the dots on one-half of a tile, he places the tile perpendicular to the line. See Figure 11-3.

Scores are kept by crediting the player with the total which his tile yields. The game ends when each player has used as many of the eight tiles as possible.

The game can be varied by changing the multiple name as Multiples-of-Two Dominoes, Multiples-of-Five Dominoes, etc. Children should be aware that they are practicing addition and multiplication as they play. There is an additional reason for alerting children to the learning objectives of a given game. Contrast the public relations value of two possible answers to the parental query, "What did you do in school today?"

"Not much. The teacher let us play dominoes in the afternoon."

"We practiced math facts in a new dominoes game."

A more theoretical rationale for alerting children to your objectives is the belief of many educators that learning is easier and more probable when the learner understands the objectives of a given educational experience.

Selecting Games for the Classroom

You will probably be encouraging children to bring games from home for use during recreation time. Read the directions for these

Multiples-of-Three Dominoes
Figure 11–3

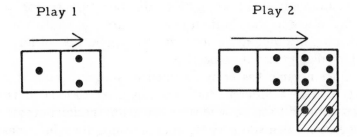

Play 1

Player scores 3 points

Play 2

Player scores 9 points

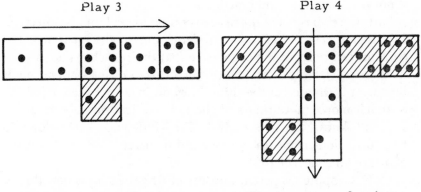

Play 3

Player scores 18 points

Play 4

Player scores 9 points

games and play the games with the children if possible, to get an idea of educational possibilities. Is it a captivating game or is it dull? How do children react to it? Can it be played during a relatively short period of time? How many children are required to play? Are there some definite verbal or mathematical learnings inherent? Are thinking skills such as predicting possible outcomes, logical analysis, or cause and effect relationships required?

When you have answered questions of this kind, some of the games will qualify for inclusion as educational media. Most will probably remain simply good recreational activities.

Having settled upon the inclusion of a specific game, you will want to introduce its formal learning value to the children. This is best done in small groups. Explain your purposes for using the game, watch as the children play, and arrange with them to stop the play in order to demonstrate the application of any strategy which reenforces your objective.

Once a game has been included in your program, it must be regarded in a different light than as a recreational device. Perhaps you will set up a separate area for special purpose games The care which you exercise in establishing the educational value of game media will frequently be reflected in the positive attitudes and learnings of children and the maintenance of good public relations. Two teachers might serve as examples of this point. Both share a similar philosophical point of view and each has attempted to enrich the classroom environment with new and innovative materials and practices.

"Mr. Care" has taken the necessary time to explain his objectives in rather specific ways to his students and to their parents. His students can relax in the confidence that their teacher knows what he is doing. A typical comment from a parent of his student might be, "Isn't it wonderful the things they do in school these days! It's so much more interesting and the kids are learning about things I didn't know until recently." The confidence cycle flows in both directions from teacher to child to parent and enhances the efforts of all concerned.

"Mrs. Groping" is perhaps unsure of why she adopts new things. She fails to communicate her objectives to students or to parents. A typical remark made by one of her student's parents might be, "Things were different when I went to school; we worked and we knew that school was for learning. My kids fool around a good part of every day. They'd be better off at home. Half the time when I ask what he learned in school that day, my son doesn't know." The cycle of insecurity is insidious in this case, and is reflected in a rather chaotic classroom, a confused teacher, and children who, lacking confidence in themselves and their teacher, are frequently covertly if not overtly belligerent.

SUMMARY

Varied media of all kinds should be used to spark and vitalize the learning programs which we plan for children. Care in planning can legitimize our use of toys and games which may well be the most attractive media that we offer to children.

At the primary level, manipulative toys and devices are ideal nonverbal tools to advance readiness for formal instruction in encoding and decoding.

The effectiveness of any media will be dependent upon the quality of the objective which we hope to attain. At the early primary level these objectives are easily seen, and our expectations of young learners make the use of toys and games acceptable as learning devices.

Beyond the primary level it is perhaps more difficult to plan learning sequences which utilize this type of media, not because the media is lacking but because we are conditioned to expect learning to come from more traditional materials. Effective utilization then requires that the teacher consciously study the inherent learning possibilities of toys and games, plan to capitalize on these inherent possibilities and to guide youngsters to attain and realize these learnings. Clarifying your objectives to children and their parents will serve to advance appropriate learnings and to develop a climate of confidence important to your classroom environment and to positive home-school relations.

TWELVE

The "Other" Children

"When you are working with a small group of children what happens to the other children?" This question is frequently asked of teachers who devote a large portion of the day to individual and small group instruction. What to do with the other children certainly becomes an immediate concern when you begin to differentiate instruction. Strictly speaking, most of the suggestions for independent and self-directing activities which have already been discussed help to answer this question. This chapter will be devoted specifically to examining attitudes and environmental arrangements necessary for providing constructive and meaning ful activities for children to engage in when you are occupied with a small group. It will suggest ways of providing on-going opportunities for independent and self-directed learning.

THE CHILD AS A SELF-DIRECTING LEARNER

We often tend to do too much organizing and directing of chi1 dren's learning experiences. We tell them which books and pages to read and which questions to try to answer. We tell them when to read, when and what to do in arithmetic, how to practice spelling, and what to expect in science experiments. No wonder there are so many children who don't know what to do with themselves when they finish one assignment and are waiting for the teacher

154

to tell them what they will be doing next. A change of attitude on the part of the teacher is necessary before we can expect a change in attitude and behavior on the part of the child. Children can be more self-directing and independent if we will let them be. But it is essential for the teacher to communicate, both verbally and nonverbally, his conviction that children can select, carry out, and evaluate worthwhile learning activities if provided with opportunities to do so.

It will be necessary for you to continue to select and direct some of the activities children engage in, of course. You will want to provide for readiness, practice, and follow-up of specific aspects of the children's instructional programs. But it is highly desirable for you to encourage as much self-selection and self-direction for each child as he can utilize to advantage. This means providing opportunities which permit children to develop independence.

These opportunities require providing children with the *time* to select and use materials as well as with the materials from which they can make selections. Have available in your classroom as many varied and provocative materials for the children to use and investigate as you possibly can. Then permit an increasing amount of time for them to select their own activities. Individual and group opportunities for self-evaluation will be helpful in setting goals and developing criteria for behavior.

Habits and Attitudes Conducive to Self-Directed Learning

As a child becomes increasingly capable of self-direction in school, he develops certain habits of learning and attitudes toward learning. Motivation for learning undergoes a change of base. He shows signs of relying on his own judgment and improves in his judgment-making abilities. Making errors takes on new meanings for him. He develops more consideration for the needs of others in the classroom. He begins to view his own learning needs and achievements more realistically. All of these modifications in thought and behavior are part of and necessary for the independent, self-directed learner.

Motivation. Motivation becomes more intrinsic. Impetus for learning depends less and less upon some system of external rewards or punishments such as a teacher's smile of approval and a good grade on a report card or a teacher's frown, a bad grade, and extra homework. (Have you noticed how often children care very little about what they are learning and see very little reason for it, but work hard because they want an A?) The child who has experienced success in learning "on his own" something which he has selected himself, becomes intrigued with the prospect that there is more to this school business than just doing what the teacher tells you to do. The enthusiasm that develops when a child is permitted to study something which is important to him, for as long as he wishes, is an enthusiasm which often results in an amazing scope and depth of learning.

One sixth-grade girl was interested in studying about American Indians. This was not a part of the regular social studies curriculum for sixth grade and many teachers would have overlooked her interest in order to "get through the sixth-grade book" by June. This girl was fortunate. Her teacher gave her the opportunity to pursue this interest on her own. He did not attempt to *teach* her anything about American Indians. He did provide her with time in the classroom and time excused from the classroom to go to the school library to read and research as her interests directed her. As a result she read more than 100 books on Indians, and several encyclopedia articles including one of 33 pages and another of 57. She wrote to the U.S. Department of Interior for pamphlets and information, kept an extensive notebook, voluntarily prepared both oral and written reports, and carried out numerous related projects at home as well as at school. These projects included chipping arrowheads and knife blades from native rocks and building a 10 by 12 foot teepee in the side yard. She also had the triumph of proving to her father (who teaches junior high social studies) that she knew more about the Indians of the Iroquois Nation than was included in his junior high curriculum.

In addition to her independent study of this self-selected topic, she was included in the regular social studies program planned by her teacher. The study of Indians was undertaken at times when the teacher was working with other groups.

As motivation becomes more intrinsic and less extrinsic, competition takes on new dimensions. The child is more interested in competing with himself and less interested in competing with others. He learns to capitalize upon his strengths and compensate for or overcome his weaknesses. He finds it more meaningful to compare his achievement with his own ability than to compare his achievement with that of others who have different strengths and weaknesses. Intrinsic motivation also tends to direct competitive feelings toward the material being studied rather than toward arbitrarily predetermined adult standards. In other words, the child wants to master a task because *he* wants to learn the material. He is challenged by the task he has selected for himself and does not feel he must compete with what the teacher has decided he must learn or do. This type of competition leads even the slowest learner and lowest achiever to a discovery of the joy of learning.

Errors. Sometimes the activities selected by a child will be of the type requiring responses to questions or problems. The child who engages in self-directed and self-corrected learning activities soon realizes that making errors is neither something to fear nor something of which to be ashamed. He should be encouraged to think of his errors as signals. The frequency of error can be looked upon as a possible indication of the appropriateness of the task he has undertaken. Too many errors might mean the material or task is difficult. It could also point to carelessness or misunderstanding of directions. The lack of error could signal that the child is ready for something more challenging. Some error is to be expected when working with new ideas and processes and the child should look upon this as a natural part of learning. He should find that the frequency of error decreases as his understandings and skills increase until a continued lack of error signals mastery of the task.

The self-directed learner needs to be shown how to analyze his errors so he can learn from them. Have him develop the habit of analyzing each error as soon as he realizes it is an error.

Did he misunderstand the question or instruction?

Was he being careless?

Is there some skill or knowledge he must learn before he is ready for the task?

Does he need to read the material more carefully?

Is the material too difficult for him?

Was it a simple matter of misinformation or a mistaken notion which has now been cleared up by virtue of seeing the correct answer?

Was he really concentrating on his work or was something distracting him?

There is a basic difference between a child's *checking* his work and a child's *correcting* his work. *Checking* involves comparison with an answer key, indicating where errors have been made, and, possibly, copying the correct response. *Correcting* includes all this plus the analysis of why or how the errors have been made. The latter is more likely to lead to greater learning and result in fewer repeated errors.

A child who merely checks his work is willing to accept the authority of the answer key. This is not always true of the child engaging in analytical self-correction. There are very good reasons for encouraging children to question the authority of the answer key. First, the answer key may be incorrect or only partly correct. The child's response may be the correct one or equally as correct as the one given in the key. Second, the child may be having difficulty in analyzing his own mistakes. Having children feel free to come to you and disagree with the answer key enables you to pinpoint such difficulties early. Questioning the authority of the answer key suggests that the child has a reason for thinking his answer is better than the one given in the key. This in turn means the child has had to analyze his response as well as the one listed as correct. Being permitted to disagree in this way encourages children to go beyond checking and engage in analytical correction. Any of these advantages of questioning the authority of the answer key is likely to result in greater learning.

Self-evaluation goes a step farther than self-correction. In self-evaluation the child analyzes patterns in his learning behavior. When he notices that he often makes errors for the same reason—not understanding instructions or not reading the material carefully—he recognizes a basic weakness in his study habits. This is part of self-evaluation. The child who compares his rate and level of progress with what he knows he is capable of is engaging in self-evaluation. So is the child who analyzes his progress, establishes new goals, and plans the next step in his study. Such self-evaluation does not always need to be highly formalized or burdened with required verbalization. Exchanging a book that is "too hard" for one that can be read, or deciding mentally, "I know all I want to about this, now I'll read about something else," are simple forms of self-evaluation. However, some directed experiences in self-evaluation are needed by most children. These can take place during pupil-teacher conferences. The frequency and depth of this directed self-evaluation will vary among children, of course. This is something you will have to determine as you observe and work with each child.

Consideration for Others. Any attempt to provide an atmosphere and environment for self-directed learning activities must provide for children to develop consideration for others. Teachers are all aware of the need for a quiet atmosphere for study, and it is not unusual for classroom rules to include "don't whisper without permission" and "raise your hand if you want to leave your desk." While they are sometimes necessary, such rules have certain limitations for programs and instructional strategies such as those described in this book

1. They represent teacher-made or teacher-elicited and teacher-imposed regulations and do not necessarily indicate a con sideration for and understanding of the needs of others on the part of the children.
2. They do not take into account the need for pupils to confer or to move about obtaining and putting away materials while engaged in independent and self-directing activities.
3. They require passive rather than active self-control and self-discipline.
4. They assume that quiet is always the appropriate atmosphere for learning.

A thoughtful examination of these limitations in the context of our objectives for individualized instruction will lead us to search for better ways of maintaining classroom control. Certainly orderly conduct resulting from self-disipline and a concern for the needs of others is highly desirable. But *how* do we accomplish such a feat? Unfortunately there are no guaranteed prescriptions to follow, but there are some guidelines which can give direction to your efforts.

Children, because of their tendency to imitate, learn from the model you establish.

Children will imitate your *behavior* more readily than they will follow your *advice* on how they should behave. If you keep your voice low, move quietly about the room, wait beside a child until you have his attention rather than interrupting his work, and if you go to the child you wish to speak to rather than disturbing the whole class by calling out your message aloud, the children will be likely to follow your example.

Children who have experienced a need are more likely to understand another's similar need than children who have not had such an experience.

Perhaps you can structure situations which point out the need for quiet at certain times. Suppose two or three children have a tendency to talk too loudly when working together and don't seem to realize how this can disturb others. You might arrange for them to engage in an activity which requires relative quiet—listening to an exciting story being read on a record, for example—during a time when the room is quite noisy with other activities. When they show signs of having difficulty hearing the story or if they comment on the noise, tell them that you will find a quieter activity for the rest of the class in just a few minutes so they can have the quiet they need to listen to the record. Then at a later time when their own noisy behavior disturbs others remind them of their experience in needing quiet.

Children usually resent and are embarrassed by public reprimand and disipline.

Resentment and embarrassment are not emotions that lead to cooperation and consideration for others. The teacher who reprimands or disciplines a child in front of his peers is guilty of lack of consideration for that child. When it is necessary to discuss a child's behavior, do it with him privately. Treat the discussion as two-way communication, not as a one-way tirade. Quite often a child who has misbehaved feels his behavior was justified. Don't just bawl him out and let him know that you "don't ever want to see him acting that way again." Let him tell you why he acted as he did and then you can suggest more acceptable ways of resolving similar situations. Agree with him, if you can, that he did indeed have a problem situation to work out, but discuss with him alternative methods for solving his problem in which others would not suffer or be disturbed. Try to turn the discussion into a plan of action for future situations. Then be sure you notice any signs of improvement and comment on them to him, privately, at appropriate times.

Children often seem to have a deep concern for fairness.

"But it isn't fair!" How often have you heard this lament? Sometimes it is merely a child's bid to get something he wants. But often it stems from a deep-seated conviction of what is fair for others as well as for himself. You can capitalize on this concern for fairness.

Plan a few small group discussion activities based on various aspects of the concept of fairness. What does it mean to be fair? What do rules and fairness have to do with each other? When something is fair, does it *have* to be fair for *everyone?* These discussions could be followed by a teacher-led discussion based on questions such as these:

Is it fair for me (the teacher) to expect you always to be very quiet in the classroom? Why do you feel that way?

When is it fair for you to expect to be able to make noise in the classroom?

How much noise is fair?

When is it fair to expect you to be quiet in the classroom?

When is it fair for one or two persons to do whatever they wish?

What classroom conditions would it be fair to expect in each of these situations:

—silent reading time?

—independent study time?

—pupil-team study time?

—small group discussion periods?

—project work time?

—testing periods?

—science experiment periods?

—free study time?

INSTEAD OF SEATWORK

A group of six primary teachers and one resource teacher worked together to find interesting and worthwhile alternatives to the steady diet of repetitious seatwork that is so often given to children to keep them occupied while the teacher meets with reading and math groups. These teachers first held a series of planning discussions during which ideas were brainstormed, requirements identified, and priorities established. A general plan emerged which called for the implementation of several interest centers in each classroom. Materials and activities to be placed in each center must meet certain criteria.
They must:

1. Require few or no written directions.
2. Be highly manipulative and concrete (as opposed to symbolic and abstract).
3. Be self-correcting or require no specific answer or response.
4. Be provocative, encouraging the child to explore, investigate, and manipulate.
5. Be curriculum related.
6. Be easy for young children to obtain, use, and put away.

The planning sessions were followed by several work periods during which some materials and equipment were gathered and others were made or supplemented by additional teacher-made materials. A schedule was drawn up which called for rotation of materials among the six teachers. This provided for a gradual turnover of activities within a given classroom. Having a continuous supply of fresh activities helped to maintain a high level of interest among the children. The schedule also made it possible to share one-of-a-kind items. The teachers then helped each other solve the problems of space and room arrangement which faced them all as they installed the six interest centers in each room. These centers included a Science Corner, a Listening Center, a Math Table, an Art Area, a Pattern and Puzzle Place, and a Special Attraction.

Finally, after more than two months of planning and preparing, I C Day arrived. Interest Center Day marked the day when the children were first introduced to the interest centers and the activities in them. Each teacher introduced the centers and established ground rules for their use in the way that best suited her own style of teaching. The general plan called for each teacher to provide every child with some time during the day when that child could engage in activities of his choice from any of the interest centers. This time was to be provided in place of some of the usual seatwork activities.

Games and activities which required training were introduced to the children by the resource teacher as soon as one of these games had been rotated into a classroom. This left the classroom teacher free to continue with small group instruction.

The interest centers were instantly and almost phenomenally successful. Teachers who had expressed concern about the effect interest centers would have on classroom control were amazed to find that there were virtually no such problems. Children were delighted to be able to choose freely from such a fascinating array of activities. Both teachers and children began to notice connections between some of the games and certain aspects of math. It wasn't long before other primary teachers in the school were asking to start interest centers in their classrooms. A second flurry of planning and preparing activity began and soon an additional seven primary classrooms had similar interest centers in operation. Intermediate teachers began planning and establishing more sophisticated adaptations of the interest center idea for the older children.

There is really nothing new about having interest centers in classrooms. Two aspects of the project described above made it somewhat unique, however. One was the cooperative planning, working, and sharing among teachers. The second was the way in which the interest centers were used—as *part* of the daily work rather than merely "after you have finished all your work."

Some of the suggestions given below were drawn from the interest centers just discussed. Others are more suitable for older children. You will undoubtedly think of many variations and additional ideas for your own interest centers.

Science Corner

Place one or two equal-arm balances in your science corner. At first let the children think of things to weigh and balance and ways to do it. Later you might add a tray of items as units of weight; dry beans, paper clips, marbles, walnuts, macaroni, wooden beads, toothpicks, etc. You might wish to post a sign reading *What will balance this?* and display a new object every two or three days. Objects to balance might include a kitchen sponge, a ruler, a wooden block, a small toy, or a piece of chalk. A chart similar to the one shown in Figure 12-1 will enable the children to record various solutions to the same problem.

What Will Balance This?		
This	Will Balance This	Discovered by
2 walnuts and 3 beads	sponge	David R.
5 beads and 4 beans	sponge	Janie S.

Figure 12–1

Cut and paste, or copy, from a variety of science books the short sections which suggest experiments for children to try. Put each experiment suggestion on a 5 x 8 inch card. Add a few questions to stimulate thinking and suggest further experimentation. Materials needed for the experiments can be labeled and stored where they are easily accessible. Set aside an area where partially completed experiments can be kept intact.

Provide space for children to display collections or to keep frogs, insects and other live specimens. Have cages, aquariums, and terrariums for the children to use. Papier mâché egg cartons, shallow cardboard containers, and sheets of corrugated cardboard are use ful for display and mounting purposes. Label-making materials such as oak tag, construction paper, and felt tip markers should also be available.

Math Table

Your math table should contain as many manipulative materials as you can find or make. Many commercial counting, place value, and numeration devices are on the market. Put your flannel board and felt cutouts where children can use them to make up and solve problems visually. Flash cards and game type activities about number facts, fractions, and telling time are available commercially or are relatively easy to make. Many games can be devised for use with a numberline. Get the children busy at the task of making up these games. The Elementary Science Study *Attribute Games and Problems** provide a rich source of ideas and materials for game type activities. Many of the math games by Wff'n Proof contain suggestions for beginning activities which can be played by elementary school children. Many publishers and school supply houses show games and devices that could be used at your math table.

It is wise not to place all of your materials at the math table simultaneously. Start out with a variety of games, manipulatives, and other devices selected from your supply. After a few

---

*ATTRIBUTE GAMES AND PROBLEMS series by Elementary Science Study. Published by Webster Division, McGraw-Hill Book Company. Copyright © 1967 1968 by Education Development Center, Inc.

weeks you might remove one or two of these and replace them with new materials. By changing just a few items every week or so you can keep the interest of most children at a high level.

Prehistoric Animal Race. One numberline game designed for use at the primary grade interest centers also has possibilities for intermediate grades. A numberline extending from 0 to 120 was taped to a counter at the back of the classroom. (The floor would do just as well.) The numberline served as the board on which the game was played. Several small plastic prehistoric animal toys were used as "men." A single die was rolled to determine the number of spaces a player would move his man. Two children were needed to play the game and as many as six could be accommodated at one time.

At first all races started at zero on the numberline. If a player rolled five on the die, he moved forward five spaces. The winner was either the player who first arrived at 120 or the player who was farthest ahead when time was up. Later, specific instructions for *Today's Race* were posted above the numberline. One day the starting line might be at 28 and the finishing line at 74 with each count of the die worth two spaces. Another day the starting line might be at 96, the finishing line at 39, and each count of the die worth three spaces.

For intermediate children a fractional numberline, a negative numberline, or a base six numberline might be used. A variety of small toys could serve as men—whatever might capture the fancy of the children. Variations on the Prehistoric Animal Race could be designed for use with the same 0 to 120 numberline with daily instructions of a more complex nature. For example, a race might start at 30 and limit the game to ten plays per child with each count of the die worth $2x-3$ spaces. Thus, depending on the count of the die, a player might move either forward or backward.

Set Formation. This is an independent activity for children to work on alone. A pack of picture cards, a pack of *set description cards*, and a pack of *set listing cards* comprise the materials needed. These are made by the teacher but can utilize picture cards from various commercial games and activities. The child spreads out the picture cards, face up. He then draws one set description card from the pack. His task is to select the appropriate picture cards and form the set described on the card he just drew. The set description card might tell him to form the set of

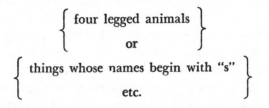

$$\left\{ \begin{array}{c} \text{four legged animals} \\ \text{or} \end{array} \right\}$$

$$\left\{ \begin{array}{c} \text{things whose names begin with "s"} \\ \text{etc.} \end{array} \right\}$$

When he has formed the set, he finds the set listings card which is numbered the same as the set description card. The set listing card serves as an answer key, so the child may check his work and go on to the next description card.

Variations on this activity can turn it into a game for two or more players. Let the children think of some ways to do this.

Other Centers of Interest

In your *Art Area* you will want to provide a variety of art media for exploration and creation. Be sure there are surfaces to work on and plenty of storage place for materials and partially finished projects. A scrapbook showing pictures of children's and adults' art work can serve as a source of ideas. Ideas might also be posted on a bulletin board showing many kinds of puppets one time and art prints or collages another. Magazines containing art ideas pages can be marked and conveniently displayed. The children will enjoy having you provide something a bit different from time to time—scraps of wrapping paper or wood, egg cartons, colorful paper bags, unusually shaped stones, assorted pieces of linoleum or floor tiles which can be cut with scissors, intriguing looking hardware, etc.

A *Creative Language Center* should provide paper, pencils, dictionaries, anthologies, and English textbooks. Scrapbooks and displays of students' work should be conspicuous. Post charts listing interesting and descriptive words which the class has "collected." Many types of pictures, story titles, and beginning sentences can be stored together in a story-idea box. Try to provide a partially isolated desk or two where your young authors can meditate and write without interruption or distraction.

You might arrange with several other teachers to plan a rotation schedule for one-of-a-kind items for your *Special Attractions* area. A puppet theater or a mock T-V set can be made from large cardboard packing boxes. A rug, a low table, and several floor pillows provide a reading retreat. A filmstrip projector and a variety of filmstrips can be used to establish a viewing center. One corner of your room could become a little theater with an improvised stage and a box of costumes and props. Five or six teachers sharing ideas and materials might be able to establish, equip, and share a small classroom kitchen, woodworking shop, grocery store, bank, or museum.

A *Patterns and Puzzle Place* may easily become one of the most popular interest centers in your room. Patterns can include sequences for construction toys like those described in the previous chapter as well as patterns and instructions for making paper hats, model airplanes, mobiles, etc. Knitting instructions and patterns for aprons or doll clothes may interest many girls. Blueprints will serve as patterns for constructing model houses or simple machines. Puzzles can include problems of logic and mathematical brainteasers as well as jigsaw puzzles, crossword puzzles, maze problems, and riddles. Games such as PYTHAGORAS® and SWITCH® puzzles are challenging additions to this interest center.* Encourage the children to bring in ideas and materials for your Patterns and Puzzle Place.

PUPIL-TAUGHT LESSONS

Often a child is something of an expert on a special topic. Why not take advantage of that child's interest and background? Let him "teach a lesson" on his topic to part or all of the class. Four to eight weeks of research and preparation should precede the lesson and should be done as independent work. Sometimes two or three youngsters might work together to plan and present a pupil-taught lesson.

---

*PYTHAGORAS® and SWITCH® puzzles are made by Kohner Brothers, Inc.

Some of the activities of planning, researching, and preparing for the lesson are similar to suggestions given earlier on taking notes and making visuals. After the child has settled on his topic, have him list many of the questions he thinks the class would like to have answered about his topic. Help him group these questions into a few major classifications and write a phrase which will stand for a heading for the questions in each group.

For example, a child having chosen the topic *Brazil* may have several questions such as: How hot is it there? Are there mountains? Why is there so much jungle in Brazil? What is the Amazon River like? These questions could be grouped under a heading such as *Land and Climate*. Other questions such as: How do they get rubber? What grows there? Do they have factories? and Does coffee come from Brazil? could be grouped under a heading such as *How People Make a Living*.

When this has been done, have the child set aside part of his notebook as a place to take notes for his report. There should be one page for each of the major headings. A portion of each page could be set aside for each question that falls under the heading. As the child reads books and articles he can jot down notes in the appropriate section of the appropriate page whenever he runs across a pertinent piece of information. Any information the child already has about his topic should be verified by research in reference and trade books.

After the research and background reading have been completed, the notes are already so well organized that preparing an outline for the lesson requires little more than copying the notes in outline form. The headings for the group of questions become the main topics. The questions, reworded into phrases, become subtopics. And the notes relating to each question become the details under the subtopics.

This outline can be used to help the pupil make final plans for the order and content of his lesson. Then he is ready to plan and prepare the visual materials he will use. These should be designed to illustrate specific aspects of his lesson. By having many of these materials and displaying them in the proper sequence, teaching the lesson becomes mainly a matter of explaining the visuals one-by-one.

Parents can be encouraged to help the pupil in preparing the visual materials. You, other pupils in your room, and the art or industrial arts teacher could also help in making the visuals. It is important that these materials clearly illustrate the points they are designed to illustrate. It is also important that a variey of types of visuals be prepared for any one lesson. Maps of various kinds; charts, graphs, and diagrams; models and dioramas; pictures and drawings; and overhead transparencies and slides can be used.

By the time the visuals have been designed and made, the pupil should feel very familiar with his subject. Now he needs practice in handling the materials smoothly and practice in orally explaining each one. He should have several practice sessions at home before he teaches his lesson in school.

A fourth-grade girl, upon returning from a trip to Arizona, decided to teach a lesson on Our Southwestern Deserts. She listed 20 questions which were then grouped into four classifications; Land and Climate, Animals, Plants, and People. Under the school librarian's direction, she then located every book in the library which might help her. From these she selected a dozen or more which she felt would best serve her purposes. As she read and took notes, this pupil found she was unable to answer a few of her original questions but located additional data which she felt was too interesting to overlook. This information was substituted for her unanswered questions. After organizing her notes into an outline, she decided it would be necessary to cut down on the amount of information she planned to include in her lesson. To do this she selected a few specific aspects of each of the four main topics. Visuals were prepared with the help of parents and teacher. The final lesson utilized two maps, several drawings, two dioramas, several transparencies, and a bar graph.

Map of the World. A large wall map of the world (made by projecting a world map transparency with an overhead projector) was used to point out the major desert regions of the world and discuss their common characteristics.

Three-Dimensional Map of the Southwest. This map was used to explain the effect of the mountains on the pattern of rainfall in the southwestern part of the United States and to show the location of the resulting desert areas.

Drawing of Land Forms. Flat sandy expanses and weathered rock outcroppings were shown by means of an 18 by 24 inch colored drawing.

Animal Drawings. Life-size drawings were made of six typical desert animals. Two larger than life size illustrations of a desert insect and spider were drawn. The drawings were quite accurate in detail and served as a basis for an explanation of how these animals adapt to the desert conditions.

Diorama of Cactus Plants. A large box painted on the inside with a desert landscape provided a background for this diorama. Saguaro, barrel, and prickly pear cacti were represented by papier mâché models.

Transparencies of Cactus Plants. Transparencies, one with several overlays, were used with the overhead projector to accompany an explanation of the growth pattern of a Saguaro cactus and of the way root systems and water storage systems help cactus plants adapt to desert conditions. For these transparencies, the pupil drew originals from which the teacher made transparencies.

Diorama of Irrigation System. Human adaptation to desert conditions by means of irrigation was explained and illustrated with a diorama showing mountains from which a river flowed, a dam which stored the river's water, irrigation canals and ditches which controlled the flow of water to farmlands, and an orange grove which was made possible only because of irrigation.

Graph of Agricultural Yields. A bar graph was used to show the yield per acre of five crops, comparing the United States average with that of irrigated Arizona land.

Long range independent projects such as this can be best carried out by children who have demonstrated an ability to be highly self-directing. Some teacher guidance is necessary, of course, and this can best be accomplished through pupil-teacher conferences.

What are some of the benefits of such a project for the child? Consider some of the activities he engages in.

1. He plans a long term project and organizes his thinking about what he hopes to accomplish.
2. He schedules parts of his own time and exercises self-discipline in following his schedule.
3. He uses research skills.
4. He exercises judgment about what is relevant and what is irrelevant.
5. He takes notes, organizes data, and writes an outline.
6. He evaluates his progress, comparing it with his objectives.
7. He exercises judgment in selecting for use the most valuable aspects of his data.
8. He analyzes his data to plan specific illustrative devices.
9. He designs and constructs a variety of visual media.
10. He makes an oral presentation to a group of his peers.

A SUGGESTION BOX

We often think of a suggestion box as a device used by employers to glean ideas from their employees. When used in the classroom to serve "the other children," the suggestion box is a device used by the pupils to glean ideas from the teacher. The suggestion box may literally be a box, or it may be a list, a chart, or a pack of cards. The main requirement is that it contain as many suggestions as possible for independent and free time activities. A wide variety of types of activities is the key to the success of this plan. The following ideas might be adopted or adapted for your suggestion box.

How many names can you think of for "12" (such as 3+9 or 24÷2)?

Make up a crossword puzzle using words about summer: play, swim, picnic, camp, etc.

Start a word chart using one of these titles: Size Words, Color Words, Space Words, Christmas Words, Action Words, etc.

My name begins with "K." Draw me.

Can you think of 25 words beginning with the "sl" blend? Put your list on the bulletin board by the door. Be sure to sign it.

Invent a new game for two to four players.

Make a chart of pictures about one of these: Things we do with water; Things that make pleasant sounds; Art all around us; etc.

Copy a poem you like on the chalkboard. Be sure to write the title and poet's name.

How many equivalent fractions can you think of for $\frac{1}{2}$? $\frac{1}{3}$? $\frac{1}{4}$?

Here are some cards with paragraphs from a story. Can you put them in order and read the story?

Use the secret code on this card to decode this message.

The line drawn on this paper is part of a picture. Can you draw the rest of the picture?

Can you make a model of an irrigation canal system?

Can you write on a card a way to find out what things are necessary to make seeds grow?

Use this code to write a message to a friend of yours. Give it to your friend after school and see if he can read it.

What can you make using a paper towel, yarn, crayons, colored paper, and a clothespin from the box on the back shelf?

Here are some cards with pictures and some with words. Can you match each picture with the word that tells who would use the thing in the picture?

Select one of the tapes of math brain teasers and use it with the earphones.

Design a bulletin board about things we might see under the sea. Submit your plans to the teacher.

Science Suggestions

You might want to have a suggestion box devoted to activities related to a single subject area. A wealth of ideas for a Science Suggestion Box can be found in children's magazines, science texts and trade books, and teacher resource books. Children who are especially interested in science could form a Science Club and actively search for new ideas for the suggestion box. Here are some possibilities to get you started.

Make a working model of a:

dam	telephone
water wheel	thermometeı
hand pump	barometeı
canal lock	wind vane
telegraph sending set	elevator

Plan a demonstration to illustrate:

how a volcano erupts
how sedimentary rock forms
how fossils form
soil erosion
osmosis
why we have day and night and seasons
how coal (or oil) is formed
capillary action in a plant

Design a take-apart-put-together toy for a young child.
Design a mechanical toy.
Design an electrically operated game.
Design an animal card game that could be played something like *Authors*.

Make a diorama of:

a limestone cave
a prehistoric undersea scene
inside a space ship
hibernating animals
life under the microscope

Plan an experiment that would answer:

Is dissolving salt in water a chemical or a physical change?
Can we speed up the time it takes a bean seed to sprout?
Can the weight of air be changed?

Design a bulletin board (submit plans to your teacher) about:

> Uses of Water
> Problems Facing Moor Pioneers
> Insects
> Elements and Compounds
> Air Pollution
> The Five Senses
> Weather
> Parts of a Flower

Design and make a poster about:

Safety	Hygiene
Conservation	Nutrition

SUMMARY

There is an immediate need for the teacher who works much of the time with small groups of pupils to provide interesting and worthwhile activities for the "other children." Your pupils should be encouraged and permitted to become self-directing and independent for an increasingly large portion of their school day. It is necessary for you to provide the atmosphere, many provocative materials, and the time needed for free selection and exploration. As children become more self-directing, motivation, competition, making errors, evaluation, and ground rules begin to have new meanings for them. A multitude of continuing opportunities for independent and self-directed learning activities can be provided through the establishment of various interest centers, through provision for pupil-taught lessons,, and by means of a well-stocked suggestion box.

THIRTEEN

Individualizing Homework

Homework fits into a program of individualized instruction just as does any other learning experience. You must plan homework to help meet specific objectives for specific children, and you must design it to be challenging enough but not too frustrating for the child who is to do it. Tasks involving reading, thinking, or study skills which a child cannot handle independently are as unrealistic for homework assignments as they are for classroom activities.

Just as there is no magic age for beginning to read, there is no magic age for beginning to have homework. Homework for some children can start as early as kindergarten or nursery school . . . "Bring in a picture and we'll make up a story about it," or "Count and find out how many spoons are on the table when you eat dinner tonight." *Who* would get assignments like these? Those children who need opportunities to enlarge their speaking and listening vocabularies might benefit from talking about pictures they find at home. Counting spoons could be appropriate for some children needing more practice in oral counting.

A Precautionary Reminder

Two misuses of homework are so prevalent as to demand comment here.

Many teachers use homework as an evaluation device—giving an assignment, checking and grading it, and using the score in averaging a grade for periodic reporting to parents. Children should be encouraged to utilize capable, reliable adults and older children as resource people—people who can assist, clarify, or check their homework for them if they wish. Many children do this even without encouragement. Homework should be acknowledged by the teacher, of course, but it should serve as a learning experience. If you want to check up on the child's learning or evaluate his prog ress, do this in the classroom. Don't use homework assignments for this purpose if for no other reason than that you cannot be sure that the work has been done completely independently.

The second misuse of homework presents an even more subtle danger. This is the tendency of many teachers to give assignments before the children are ready for them. Assignments designed to give practice in a skill, for the purpose of increasing speed or extending the skill horizontally can be very valuable *providing the child has also mastered the process involved* in the practice exercises.

For example, suppose that a child who knows his multiplication facts through 9 x 5 has been shown how to solve multiplication examples involving regrouping, or carrying. It could be a tragic misuse of homework to ask this child to go home and do a page of examples such as:

$$\begin{array}{ccc} 76 & \text{or} & 429 \\ \times 4 & & \times 3 \end{array}$$

He might be able to do them, but he might not yet have mastered the process—the "how" to multiply with regrouping. The assumption that because he has mastered the facts through 9 x 5 and has been exposed to the process, he is now ready to do homework with these facts and this process may result in the child's becoming completely confused about the process and therefore frustrated with it. He may end up "practicing his mistakes" unless the teacher is sure he is sufficiently independent with the process. Mastery of the facts and capability to apply the process are both necessary before homework assignments of the type described would be beneficial. Such homework assignments could give him practice in using the skill to increase his speed. Or, if he had learned the process using only the multiplication facts through 9 x 4, he could now be reasonably expected to be able to extend the skill horizontally, to use facts through 9 x 5—facts which he already knows—in the same kind of example.

Occasionally you will find a child or a few children who are unusually able to benefit from self-evaluation. These are the children who will investigate their own errors and track down the reasons for them, thus learning through self-correction. Such children might be able to handle the kind of homework described above a little sooner than other children if they were given answer keys showing all of the steps in the new process and encouraged to check each example carefully before going on to the next.

HOMEWORK FOR EACH CHILD

Giving a homework assignment to each child is not the same thing as giving all the children a homework assignment. The latter can be interpreted as meaning a single assignment which all children will do. Homework for each child implies differentiation, although this does not necessitate a completely unique assignment for each and every child in your room. As with other aspects of a program of individualized instruction, you should attempt to vary the length, type, and frequency of homework according to the things you know about the children.

Not all classrooms are endowed with a variety of multilevel materials from which to assign work. Often the teacher finds it necessary to "make do" with 30 copies of a single text. This is especially likely to be true of math, English, and social studies materials. A great deal more ingenuity is required to differentiate homework assignments in such cases, but it can be done.

Differentiating with a Single Textbook

Let us suppose that a teacher is about to start a new social studies unit on the Far East. Each child has been issued a copy of a textbook which has a unit entitled "The Far East." What are some things this teacher could do with this textbook to plan homework assignments for some of the individual differences in his classroom?

For those children whose level of reading skills is too low to allow them to read the text, he might plan this assignment: "Look at the illustrations in this unit. Make a list of the pages which have illustrations that will tell us something about the ways in which the people of the Far East make a living. Make another list of pages with illustrations that tell us something about the kinds of homes (or transportation, or food, or climate, or customs, etc.) found in this part of the world."

For those children who have difficulty organizing the reading they do into any kind of pattern or sequence of ideas, he might plan an assignment such as this to precede any reading of the text. —"Make a list (or an outline) of all the topics and subtopics in this unit of the text." Later he might ask this group just prior to reading a section of the text, to discuss the kinds of information they think might be in that section.

Another group might be asked to scan for vocabulary words that will need to be explained or researched. Still others might be asked to preread a given section and write a few questions which can be answered when that section is under study. One or two might be asked to read a particular part of the unit and prepare a display to illustrate it. A small group could be asked to survey the unit and plan a bulletin board. Some rather advanced students might be asked to design questions about a given illustration which would emphasize a particular concept such as similarities and differences between the Far East and the United States, or ways in which the people utilize or are limited by their environment. One especially good reader could be asked to practice reading orally a section of the unit which he will then record on tape to be used by some of the class at a later time. Such homework assignments could be of an ongoing nature and would probably not be of the overnight variety.

Something for the Classroom

One way to help overcome the lack of instructional materials in your classroom is to let the children make some as part of their homework program. This type of assignment is not only fun, but also has real meaning for the children because they know there is a need for the material and because they will see the materials they produce actually being used as part of the instructional program. The suggestions for pupil-prepared math materials given below also provide the children with practice in computation.

Making Math Materials. The two assignments suggested here will provide you with multilevel materials in problem solving and with materials for independent study of basic arithmetic "facts."

1. Give each child several 4" x 6" slips of paper and a duplicated copy of a sign advertising a toy sale and listing several items with regular and sale prices. See Figure 13-1.

Toy Sale

Item	Regular Price	Sale Price
Large Dolls	$5.49	$3.98
Small dolls	2.99	1.75
Trucks	3.50	2.69
Balls	1.00	.87
Airplanes	1.79	1.20

Figure 13–1

Ask each child to take these items home with him and to make up several arithmetic problems based on the data on the toy sale sign. Only one problem should be written on a slip of paper. The solution to the problem and the child's name should be shown on the back of the paper. Ask each child to make up at least three "hard" problems.

At first this may not seem like individualized homework; every child has been given the same assignment. But in this case, differentiation of expectation provides the individualization. You will have set different standards of acceptability for various children. What constitutes a "hard" problem for some children will be easy for others.

When the problem slips are turned in, you may have a group of able math students check them for correctness or you may wish to do this yourself. Then you will want to sort the problems according to the difficulty of the computation required. The problems should then be copied onto oak tag cards just as they appear on the slips of paper. You might have the children copy their own problems or you may want to do this yourself to insure uniformity of script. In either case, the name of the child who originated the problem should appear on the back of the card with the solution. That child then becomes the resource person to whom others may turn if they need help in solving the problem.

An enlarged copy of the toy sale sign can be posted in the room and the problem cards stored in boxes or manila envelopes nearby. Problem cards may be coded as to difficulty by number, letter or color. You may wish to assign certain children to work with a specific set of cards, while others might be given free choice. Save the problem cards and toy sale sign for another year. Even if you use the same technique again, you'll never have too much of this kind of material.

2. This activity is similar to the one just described. Only one assignment is given, but the ways in which the children approach the task and the solutions they work out will differ.

Several children who live near each other may want to work on this project together. Tell the children that the object of the assignment is to design a game, to be played alone or by two or more players, which will give practice in using addition, subtraction, multiplication, or division facts. The project is not one that can be done overnight. Days or even weeks may be needed to work out all the rules of the game. Some children will not be able to do it at all, so you might make it a voluntary assignment.

It may prove helpful to suggest several kinds of game materials from which the children may choose. Someone might make up a card game where a pack of cards of some sort is dealt out to the players. A game might be designed around a spinning device. Another could use flash cards as the basic material. Still another could use a game board as the basis of play. Once the children begin to think creatively about the task, they will probably amaze you with the games they design.

Art Lending Library. Here is a project which results in a very worthwhile service to the class. Everyone can contribute in some way. Part of the project is done in the classroom; part as homework.

Start by leading a whole-class discussion. Talk about the lending function of libraries and about lending libraries in museums and art galleries. Suggest the possibility of establishing your own classroom Art Library. Ask for ideas about the kinds of art objects that might be included in this library. (They could be magazine pictures, real objects, children's work, etc.) Obtain ideas about art media that might be in such a library. What books, magazines, and other kinds of materials could also be included? What arrangements would need to be made for mounting, displaying, storing, and keeping track of items in the library? Then ask each child to think of one or two ways in which he could best help develop an art lending library for the class. Some might be able to donate or help search for objects to be available for loan. Others might enjoy organizing the physical facilities or designing the record-keeping forms for the library. A talent for working carefully and neatly might be utilized for mounting and framing (with oak tag or construction paper) paintings and art prints. Still others could make posters or arrange a display to advertise the library's services. People to keep records and operate the lending library would also be needed.

After the various jobs have been distributed, you could appoint two or three coordinators to be in charge of the project. Much of the actual work of establishing the library would be done as homework. Periodic progress reports to the whole class would serve as gentle reminders to those who were falling behind schedule in performing their tasks. A "grand opening" should be planned for a specific date, once it appears likely that the library will be ready for business by that time.

INDIVIDUALIZING WHOLE-CLASS ASSIGNMENTS

It has already been suggested that whole-class assignments can be individualized by differentiating the expectations we have and the standards we set for various children. There are other ways. We can differentiate the method or materials with which the assignment is to be carried out. Planning a variety of follow-up activities for a single homework assignment can also take into account individual differences within the class. A blanket type assignment can provide for each child to carry it out in ways that are personally relevant for him. An example of each of these techniques for differentiating whole-class assignments is given below

Comparative Shopping

A class engaged in a study of economic factors in our society might profit from an assignment in comparing prices of easy-to-find products. All children in the class could be asked to do some comparative shopping. The items to be compared, the degree to which children are to analyze differences in price, and the method of obtaining information about prices could be varied according to what is convenient and possible for a child to do. Here are several possibilities.

- Use this newspaper (teacher provides the newspaper, if necessary) to find the store where you could get the best buy on a five-pound bag of sugar.
- Go to at least three service stations and learn the price of regular gasoline and premium gasoline. Keep a record of the names and locations of the service stations as well as the prices of gasoline.
- What kind of bar soap do you use? Would it be cheaper to buy this soap in a super market or a drug store? Check the prices in two or three of each kind of store.
- Compare the price per ounce of the regular size jar of three different brands of instant coffee.
- Think of a brand of laundry detergent. Find the price per ounce of this detergent for each of the different size boxes in which it is sold. Which is the most economical size to buy?
- Do some window-shopping. Write down prices of several sweaters you see in store windows. Write the names of the stores next to the prices. Why might there be differences in the prices of sweaters?

Two or three children might work together on a single question, while others might work alone. Perhaps a few children would like to do more than one. Allow several days for the children to obtain their information. Then you might have them discuss their findings in small groups or as a whole class. Ask them to discuss the implications their findings might have on them as consumers, or on their families.

Measuring Things

In this assignment all children are asked to go home and measure things. Each child is given exactly the same list as every other child. Differentiation comes in the activities which follow up the homework. Thus the measuring assignment may be considered a preliminary or preparatory step. The children could be given a duplicated assignment sheet which also serves as a worksheet for recording measurements. It might also be necessary to provide rulers for some of the children. The assignment might read:

Find these things in your home. Measure them carefully. Write the measurement in feet and inches on the chart below. Draw a sketch if it will help.

Item to measure	Length	Width
1. A door		
2. A table top		
3. Your bedroom floor		
4. A picture		
5. One wall		

Follow up the measuring homework with a variety of small-group activities, assigning children to groups according to their abilities to solve the arithmetic computations involved in the activities. Such activities might be organized like this:

Group I. The children in this group could be asked to compare some of their measurements. They might compile a list of the widths of all the doors measured by their group putting them in order from the narrowest to the widest. You could also ask them to find the difference between the length of the longest wall and the length of the shortest wall. Perhaps some simple exercises in finding perimeter would be appropriate for this group.

Group II. A different approach to comparison could be the basis for this group's activity. Have the children design and make a series of bar graphs illustrating the differences in measurements. They could then prepare a package of problem cards (with solutions given on the backs of the cards) based upon the graphs. The graphs and cards could be displayed on a counter or bulletin board as part of a math interest center for others in the class to use.

Group III. A list of questions requiring the computation of area might be given to a third group. This list could include such questions as:

1. What is the area in square inches of the largest picture?
2. What is the average area in square feet of all the floors measured by the group?
3. What is the difference between the area of the largest door and the area of the smallest door?
4. What are the measurements of the two walls that are most nearly alike in area?

Group IV. One group might be asked to draw the measured items to scale. They could be asked to:

- Draw all the doors to a scale of $\frac{1}{2}'' = 1'$.
- Draw all the table tops to a scale of $2'' = 1'$.
- Draw all the walls and floors to a scale of $\frac{1}{4}'' = 1'$.
- Draw all the pictures to a scale of $4'' = 1'$.

Other Groups. Problems involving conversion of measurements to the metric system might be given to a fifth group. A few children might be asked to convert the measurements to base two. Several problem sheets could be distributed to small groups. These would contain a variety of kinds of problems to solve, each sheet with problems of a given difficulty. "How many inches of picture frame molding would be needed to frame each picture?" and "If the molding costs 14¢ an inch, how much would each frame cost?" could be on one problem sheet. Another might contain more complex problems such as "If adhesive backed vinyl is 18 inches wide and costs 49¢ per yard, what will be the cost of covering all the table tops with this material?" The difficulty of the computation involved, the complexity of the stated problem, and the number of steps required to solve the problem should all be taken into consideration when determining which problems to group together.

Time Study

You and your class could work together to plan this activity and each child could follow up the planning with his own time study assignment. You might begin by giving a brief account of one or two time studies conducted in industry or in some commercial establishment. Have the whole class experiment with the process of doing a time study by attacking some routine classroom task such as distributing supplies. Try out several methods: teacher pass out supplies to each child, teacher give supplies to several children who in turn distribute them, have a central supply counter where children help themselves, etc. Use a stopwatch to time each method several times and find the average time spent with each method. Discuss the findings.

After the class has had some group experience with timing alternative methods, have them plan a time study of their own. Each child would select one or more tasks which is his responsibility at home and design his own time study plan. You might find it necessary to make a few suggestions to start them thinking. Can two children working together make two beds faster than they can each make one bed working alone? What are some ways you can organize the work involved in setting the table so that you have to make fewer trips from the cupboards to the table, and which way actually takes the least amount of time? Perhaps several children who are going to study the same task could work as a group planning their studies and comparing notes as the studies progress.

INDIVIDUAL AND SMALL GROUP ASSIGNMENTS

As your regular instructional program becomes more and more individualized, you will find an increasing number of opportunities for giving individuals and small groups homework assignments. Most often these will come as a direct result of some activity the child is engaging in. He may need additional practice in some area or he may be ready to undertake some independent study. Perhaps he has developed a special interest in something he has been doing in class and asks for "more things like this that I can do at home." Occasionally these assignments will result from some out-of-school factor which affects the child.

Science Explorations

Science is one academic area where it is relatively easy for you to let the interests of a child determine some of the content of his science program. The processes involved in exploring and experimenting with phenomena of the physical universe can be developed with a child who is interested in electricity and things electrical as well as with one who wants to work with plants or space or rocks and minerals or insects. Taking advantage of the varied interests of the children is likely to result in a higher intensity of study and longer span of application to tasks. Assignments that capitalize on specific interests of children can be as simple as collecting and classifying leaves or as involved as designing and drawing blueprints for an intercom system. The ways in which you make these assignments can range from casual suggestions to specifically worded printed assignments.

Extending Experiments. One of the most spontaneous types of homework assignments comes as the result of obvious enthusiasm during a classroom experiment. A young child who becomes excited over a discovery about what things will or will not dissolve in water could be encouraged to extend this experiment at home in any one of several ways.

> Try some more experiments at home and see if you can add to your lists of *will dissolve* and *won't dissolve* in water.
>
> When you are at home see if heating the water will make any difference in the way things dissolve in water. Would adding ice cubes make any difference?
>
> I wonder if all these things would also dissolve in vinegar? Why don't you try it at home and see?
>
> Look at this list of things that won't dissolve in water.

I wonder if you could find other liquids around home in which some of these things will dissolve.

Problem Cards. Questions printed on problem cards can be kept on hand to give to children who are especially interested in science. Draw the questions from a variety of topics, and you will be likely to find something to interest all your science buffs. Your problem cards might include questions similar to these.

1. How does our community obtain enough safe water to supply all its needs?
2. Can you draw a diagram of the heating system in your home? Be sure to include an explanation of how it works.
3. Can you find samples of several kinds of soil in our community? Use the soil testing kit in our science cupboard to see what you can learn about your soil samples.
4. How many different kinds of animals can you see in a two-hour period? Keep a list. Make your list so that you have several groups of animals. Have all the animals in a group alike in some way. Give each group a title.
5. What makes a telephone work?
6. Sit in your bedroom and look around. How many things can you find that have come from some part of a plant? Keep a list. Can you tell what part of a plant each came from?
7. Look at the sky every night at the same time. What changes do you notice in the sky?
8. What makes a parachute work?

Scavenger Scrapbook. Children of many ages enjoy keeping a scrapbook. Perhaps some of the children in your room would enjoy being "science scavengers" to collect pictures and samples of specific science objects for a class scrapbook. Each page in the scrapbook could be given a title or caption to indicate what kind of illustration or sample belongs on the page. Pages from a scrapbook for primary children could include the following:

Shadows	Sounds We Hear
Animals with Fur	Water to Drink
Animals that Fly	Water for Plants
Plants We Eat	Water for Fun
Plants with Flowers	Seeds that Travel
Electricity at Home	Things in the Sky

Older children could hunt for illustrations like these to put on pages:

Life Cycle of a Frog	Using Magnets
Parts of a Flower	Space Travel
Pulleys at Work	Nature's Parasites
Cumulus Clouds	20,000 Leagues Under the Sea
Under the Microscope	Chemical Changes
Erosion	Kinds of Precipitation

Taking Advantage of Trips

When a youngster goes on a trip with his parents you are quite often asked to provide him with homework to take along "so he can keep up with the rest of the class." Keeping up with the rest of the class is not such a problem in a program of individualized instruction. When the child returns from his trip he merely picks up where he left off with his school work. There might be some parts of his program which he could take with him on his trip; independent reading, some practice or maintenance examples in math, self-correcting materials from any academic area, etc. But to ask him to spend very much time doing this kind of homework would not be taking advantage of the unique learning opportunities of a trip.

You could help him turn his trip into a living geography lesson by asking him to keep a Geography Log as he travels. Have him record information about the land forms and water bodies he goes past (or over). Highlights about the economic factors of cities or areas he visits should be included in the log. He could be on the lookout for farms, keeping track of all the kinds of agriculture he noticed. Perhaps, if his parents were willing, they could arrange for him to visit some farm or industry typical of the area. You might also have him use a road map to trace the route of his trip.

Other types of assignments might be possible and appropriate, taking advantage of specific features of places to be visited. A visitation to a particular museum or art gallery could be suggested. The youngster might take pictures or collect postcards showing historical or physical landmarks. Or perhaps the pictures could be

of typical plant, animal, or physical features of the area; palm trees
and flamingos in Florida or cactus plants and weathered rock for-
mations in the deserts of the Southwest. Many children become especially interested in some special feature of an area they have
visited. You may find that these youngsters could engage in some
depth study assignments about these features following their trips.

Homework on Homework

For those children whose study habits or home environments
are not conducive to carrying out homework tasks, some special
assignments about doing homework might be appropriate. Engage these children in one or two discussions about homework. Keep the focus very broad. "How do you feel about homework? Why?" or "What's the biggest problem about doing school
work at home?" Keep the atmosphere of the discussion very per-
missive. Don't pass value judgments or try to impose values at
this time. Learn as much as you can about the problems each
youngster faces when he tries to do homework.

You could follow these discussions with a special assignment.
The assignment itself is of relatively little importance here because you are more interested in having each child report back
about all the things that happened when he did that assignment.
Where did he work? What was it like where he worked? What
time was it? How long did he work on his assignment? How many
interruptions did he have? What things interrupted him? How
many times did he stop working on his assignment? What were
the reasons for stopping? How did he feel about doing the assignment?

Individual conferences would be held following this special
assignment. You should help each child identify the major difficulties he faces in doing homework. Together you can work out
a plan for attacking these difficulties. For one child it might be
searching for the quietest place to study. For another it might
be a matter of organizing his study area so he can find things when
he needs them. Finding satisfactory ways of organizing time or
developing a more positive mental *set* for study could be among
the problems facing other children.

As each child works toward solving his own special problem,

short academic assignments can be given so he can try out his proposed solution. Frequent brief conferences will be necessary throughout the undertaking. Not all children will succeed in solving their problems. Often you and the child will have to accept very small gains in improved conditions and you will want to be guided by this fact in planning additional homework for this child. You may find that for a few children, the best thing you can do is simply to stop giving them homework altogether. Perhaps these youngsters could be given a special time and place during the school day where they could work on assignments similar to homework assignments.

SUMMARY

Homework should be more than a random assortment of spur-of-the-moment ideas, left-over chores, or traditionally routine assignments. It should be a thoughtfully planned and well organized part of your program. Differentiation in homework assignments follows naturally your attempts to individualize instruction. Your objectives for a child and the conditions in his home are factors influencing your decisions about homework for that child.

Homework assignments can be differentiated even where multi-level materials are not available. You will also find it possible to provide for individual differences within the context of whole-class assignments. Opportunities to plan assignments for individuals and small groups often arise from the special interests, personal experiences, or unique needs of children. Many specific examples of ways to individualize homework have been examined.

FOURTEEN

Instructional Materials for Individualized Learning Activities

The teacher attempting to individualize the instructional program is a busy teacher and one who utilizes his time in somewhat different ways than does the more traditionally oriented teacher. You will find yourself spending less time correcting children's work and more time designing and preparing instructional materials for them to use. Commercially published self-pacing materials such as SRA Reading Laboratory® labs and social study skill kits are marketed in increasing number and variety. Some of these may be suitable for certain of your educational objectives. It is certainly to your advantage to use these whenever they are appropriate and available. However, you will find that, as you become more concerned with diagnosing the learning needs of individuals rather than of whole classes, you will become more highly selective when choosing materials to use. You will also find yourself using commercial materials in new, more creative ways.

Once you have your objectives in mind and are familiar with the various needs and levels you wish to provide for, you are ready to gather and organize the materials for these needs and levels. At first you will need to make a conscious effort to search for materials which can be adopted or adapted for your purposes. You must learn to look at old materials in new ways as well as to select appropriate items from new materials. Old worksheets can be brought into use for some children by providing keys. Arrange with teachers from other grade levels to share ditto masters so that you and they can provide for various levels in a given skill or content area. Magazine illustrations or those torn from old textbooks might become the basis for a small group to use together with the teacher's guiding questions (on a card), for making observations and inferences which will lead to concept formation and eventually to statements of generalizations. Soon you will find yourself automatically looking for the potential usableness of materials you might never have considered for instructional purposes before.

ADAPTING COMMERCIAL MATERIALS

Commercially available self-directing and self-correcting materials can often be used in part or *in toto* for some children. Textbooks from lower or higher levels can be disassembled and useful pages packaged into booklets or pasted on cards for specific purposes. There are a variety of ways in which you can use commercially preprinted duplicating masters in an individualized program.

When selecting commercial materials to use in your program, keep two points in mind. First, you must always strive to match the level, content, and prerequisite skills of a given instructional material with the abilities, skills, and needs of specific children. If the children and the materials are not well matched, little desirable learning will take place. Second, keep an open mind about commercially made materials. Even if you do not wish to use them as they have been intended, you may find there are ways of reorganizing them to make them more flexible and to allow for differences in rate and level of pupil performances.

Workbooks

Workbooks offer an excellent example of commercial materials which can be adapted and reorganized to suit a variety of purposes. Some pages from an easy reading workbook could provide a simple map about which you could prepare questions for geography skills work to be used by a group of children whose reading level prohibits using a class text or grade level workbook. Pictures cut from a numbers readiness arithmetic book might provide the raw materials for small group activities in classification.

One teacher built a resource file of multilevel practice exercises in subskill areas of reading. She gathered four copies each of reading workbooks at all levels, pre-primer through 3^2, from five basal reading series. (Four copies of each workbook yield two copies of each side of a page—one to be used to direct the pupil's activity, the other to be used as an answer key.) These workbooks were disassembled and each page studied to determine the specific subskill being practiced. Some pages were rejected and thrown away. Answer keys were made for all the others. Directions were written or rewritten when necessary. These pages of practice exercises were then packaged in acetate sheet protectors. Each acetate cover held a practice page on one side and the answer key on the other side. The acetate practice packages were then filed alphabetically by skill, and color coded by reading level.

The file was used in an individualized reading program. As the teacher held conferences with each pupil she was able to identify subskill areas which needed strengthening. After working personally with the child on the needed skill—for example, the way in which endings and suffixes change the meanings of root words —this teacher could quickly locate several appropriate practice pages at that child's independent reading level and give these to the child for independent study.

The child would write his responses to the practice exercises on a separate piece of paper. When a workbook page was completed, the acetate package was turned and incorrect answers checked with a red pencil. The practice exercise was turned again and any incorrect answers reworked. Completed work was placed in the pupil's folder awaiting the next conference. The child worked at his own rate, completing as much as he could at one time and resuming his work wherever he left off.

Similar practice packages could be prepared by pasting workbook pages on oak tag, by laminating them together, or by a dry mount process. A resource file such as this could also be made from math workbooks and used for individual independent practice in much the same way.

Duplicating Masters

When commercially made duplicating masters (or teacher-made dittoes) are used indiscriminately, we can question the validity of their inclusion in the instructional program. The teacher who distributes 30 copies of the same ditto to an entire class may very well be distributing inappropriate "busy work" to many children. However there is nothing inherent in commercial duplicating masters which demands that they be used in this man ner. When carefully selected and thoughtfully reorganized they can provide the basis for some very good multilevel self-pacing learning packages.

For example, one intermediate level teacher used the *Reading-Thinking Skills* duplicating masters published by The Continental Press, Inc. to prepare just such a set of learning packages. These materials were designed to give children practice in applying critical thinking skills to reading activities. They are available at levels from readiness through 6^2.

The teacher used the children's instructional reading levels as a guide in planning these packages. Since the materials were to be used largely as self-correcting, independent activities, he prepared packages a year below the instructional level of each child. In this way he assembled packages ranging from second-grade level through fifth-grade level. Keys were made for all exercises at each level. These keys were packaged in acetate covers and filed in a readily accessible box for use by the children. Copies of the exercises at each level were run off in quantities to provide for all children at that level. The packages were assembled, stapled together, and given to the children who kept the packages in their reading folders.

Packages were assigned to the children in various ways. Some were given packages containing all 24 pages of a given level and permitted to work, either in sequence or in random order, at their own rate. Others were given smaller packages and allowed to proceed at their own rates for a short period of time, after which the teacher would meet with them to discuss their progress and assign the next package. Only one or two pages at a time were assigned to a few of the children. This enabled the teacher to review the work with the child, at reading conferences, more frequently than he did with most children.

SUPPLEMENTING COMMERCIAL MATERIALS

Often the instructional materials with which you are provided cannot be adopted as is or even reorganized for flexible and/or multilevel use in your program. This is especially true in many cases where the instructional material is a textbook or is produced in some other nonconsumable format. School systems frown on our cutting up current textbooks. And, unfortunately, not enough text material is published in smaller, softbound form.

There may be a variety of reasons why the material you are forced to use does not meet your needs. Perhaps you wish to pursue a certain aspect of some topic to greater depth. There may be many concepts which you wish to develop which are not included in your material. You may find that provisions for practicing and applying certain skills are lacking. The material you have may not provide for differing levels of ability, differing rates of working, or differing interests. Diagnostic and mastery tests to accompany the material may be inadequate or totally lacking. Even many of the newer self-pacing and multilevel packages do not provide sufficient opportunity for diagnostic and mastery evaluation.

What can you do when you are well stocked with just such materials and when you are faced with just such limitations? Analyze carefully. Select judiciously. And supplement freely. Analyze the material you have in terms of the needs of your students and the objectives you have in mind. Select those portions of the materials which seem appropriate to use in your program. Then be as creative and as productive as you can in preparing supplemental materials to overcome some of the limitations with which you are faced.

Job Sheets

A variety of multilevel follow-up activities, in-depth studies, readiness activities, etc. can be made to supplement your materials. Job sheets, for example, can be designed to direct students to work with certain parts of the material and to skip or touch briefly on other parts. Job sheets can be used to allow some children to move more rapidly in a program or series of activities. Research and project activities can also be guided through the use of job sheets.

Job Sheet
Fractions

Check When Completed	Job No.	Materials Needed	Instructions
	1.	-Attribute Blocks -Problem Cards F-1, F-2, F-3, F-4, and F-5	Use the Attribute Blocks to solve the problems on the cards. Check with answer keys.
	2.	-Small flannel board -Envelope of felt pieces -Problem Cards F-11, F-12, F-13, F-14, and F-15	Use the flannel board and felt pieces to follow directions given on the problem cards. Check with answer keys.
	3.	-Drawing paper -Crayons -Problem Cards F-21, F-22, F-23, F-24 and F-25	Follow directions on the problem cards. Give your work to the teacher.
	4.		See the teacher for instructions.
	5.	-Math-in-acetate worksheet F-1	Write answers on your own paper. Check with answer key.

Figure 14–1

A job sheet is essentially a series of tasks to be completed by the child. These tasks are generally listed in the order in which they are to be undertaken. The job sheet should include information about the materials which will be needed for each task. Any instructions necessary for the successful performance of the task should also be given. Points at which children are to "check with the teacher" or "take a test before proceeding farther" need to be clearly indicated.

Tasks in Math. One job sheet, a portion of which is illustrated in Figure 14-1, contains a series of activities related to part of a unit on fractions. This particular job sheet was designed for a group of children who needed more work with the concept of a fraction as a name for part of a group, or set, of objects than was provided in the regular math textbook.

An example of the problems encountered with the *Attribute Blocks* includes the following instructions.

> Take all the large squares out of the box.
> How many members are there in the set of large squares? (*four*)
> How many members are there in the subset of large green squares? (*one*)
> One out of four is named by the fraction $\frac{1}{4}$. The subset of large green squares can be compared to the total number of large squares by the fraction $\frac{1}{4}$ to show that it is one of the four large squares.
> How many members are in the subset of large red squares? (*one*)
> What fraction will compare this subset to the total set of large squares? ($\frac{1}{4}$)

Similar problems would be solved by using individual flannel boards and felt pieces. The problem cards for Job No. 3 ask the children to do such things as these.

> Draw a set of six apples. Put a ring around a subset of two of these apples. Write a fraction to compare the number of the ringed apples with the total number of apples in your set.
> Draw a set of twelve stars. Color $\frac{2}{3}$ of the stars yellow.

This paper will be checked by the teacher. If additional help is needed it can be given individually or to a few children at a time. Job No. 4 will depend upon the child's success with the previous task. He may be told to skip right ahead to Job No. 5 or he may be given more problem cards similar to those already used. In the latter case, such a task would probably be given only after further teacher-directed practice with the *Attribute Blocks* and/ or flannel board. The worksheet in Job No. 5 will lead the child into using pictures (semiconcrete sets) for illustrating fractional parts of sets and will require more writing of fractions.

Study Guides

Study guides can be used to focus attention on certain aspects of a study or to help develop specific concepts. Practice in applying skills can also be provided through the use of study guides. The term study guide as it is used here refers to a kind of self-correcting worksheet which guides the learner through a short series of questions, problems, or activities and which gives him immediate feedback about the correctness of his responses. It is, therefore, a suitable format for activities requiring specific right-or-wrong answers. Questions, exercises, or problems are usually printed on the right hand side of study guides with answers listed on the left, next to the corresponding exercise. You may direct a student to fold under the answers or cover them with a marker as he works. The use of a marker simplifies checking his answers after each exercise; folding under is more satisfactory if you want the child to complete all exercises before he checks his answers. The student may write directly on the study guide or you may wish to have him use a separate sheet of paper so that the study guide may be used with another student at another time

The objective you have in mind will help you design the study guide. A study guide usually requires that the student refer to some source of information in order to be able to respond to the questions. The information may be found in a reading selection which you specify. It may be found through the study of a map, graph, picture, or chart. Perhaps the child will need to view a film or listen to a tape or record in order to be able to answer the questions. You might want him to draw from his experience or to use skills of some sort—library skills or dictionary skills, for example—in answering the questions. The purpose for which you are designing the study guide will determine which source of in-

MAP READING STUDY GUIDE

Your partner and you should talk over these items, but each of you should write answers on your own papers. Use the four maps of South America (rainfall, natural vegetation, physical-political, and population) to answer these questions.

1. Broadleaf evergreens	1. What kind of vegetation grows where there is over 60 inches of rainfall each year?
2. 40-60 inches	2. How much annual rainfall is needed for grasslands?
3. Hot and wet because it is near the equator and gets much rainfall	3. What do you think the climate would be like along the Amazon River? Why?
4. Cooler because it is higher above sea level	4 Why would the temperature be different in Ecuador?
5. Along the western coast	5. Where are the highest areas in South America?
6. Almost none	6. How many people per square mile live in the places where broadleaf evergreens grow?
7. Along the Amazon River	7. What part of the region covered by broadleaf evergreens has more people than the rest of that region?
8 Along the east coast	8. Where do most of the people in South America live?

Figure 14–2

formation you select as well as the type and sequence of exercises you formulate.

Guiding Map Reading. Figure 14-2 shows a portion of a social studies study guide. It requires the child to use certain map reading skills and to apply these skills to the study of four special purpose maps of South America—a rainfall map, a population map, a vegetation map, and a political-physical map. In order to answer most of these questions, the child must compare at least two of these maps.

Providing for Evaluation

In one school a self-pacing, multilevel package of activities designed to help children apply reading skills to content areas was being used by several intermediate teachers for some of their students. The children enjoyed using the materials and the teachers felt that the exercises were very worthwhile. But there were no evaluation instruments to use with the commercially published kits. A resource teacher analyzed the skills emphasized in each lesson for each level of the material and designed a series of 18 tests. These tests were then used at specified points throughout the various levels and categories of the instructional material. This was admittedly a major undertaking, and we know that many schools do not have a resource teacher to help with designing this kind of supplemental material. It would be possible, however, for several teachers to share the work and share the resulting tests with each other. Pooling efforts and ideas often makes a major task possible.

DESIGNING ORIGINAL MATERIALS

There will be times, of course, when you will find it necessary to design and build your own instructional materials. Whenever you find it impossible to locate commercial materials which meet your needs or which can be supplemented to meet your needs, you will need to make your own. Any of the formats discussed in Supplementing Commercial Materials can also be used for original materials.

Careful thought and planning before you start actually producing materials will save you much time and needless effort. Have
objectives for your materials clearly in mind and very often the
content will unfold naturally. Assess the levels at which various
children can work. Plan to have your materials structured ac-
cordingly. You will need to decide if a few exercises will serve your
objectives adequately. Or will it be necessary to plan an ongoing
program of some kind requiring a sequence or long series of exercises? You will find it to your advantage to design self-directing
and self-correcting materials whenever possible, but remember
to include evaluation devices from time to time. You will probably
want to allow for teacher-directed and teacher-introduced activities as well as for materials for independent study. Careful attention to these questions and planning aspects of making materials
will simplify the actual design and production of the materials.

Graph Reading Exercises

A fourth-grade teacher wished to prepare a series of graph reading exercises for a group of her students. The children for whom
she planned the materials could work independently at grade
level in reading and had sufficient problem-solving and computa-
tional skills in arithmetic to enable them to handle two-step and
three-step problems. They were quick to catch on to new ideas
and new activities in math. All of these children had experienced
making and using bar graphs. The teacher decided that these
children would probably need only one or two teacher-led introductory lessons illustrating how data can be shown on various
kinds of graphs and some brief oral experience in solving problems
by using data obtained from these graphs. She felt that it would
not be necessary to overburden these students with self-correcting
activities to follow up the introductory lessons.

This teacher designed and made a series of twelve graph reading study guides; two called for solving problems using data found
in picture graphs, four used bar graphs, three used single-line
graphs, and three used double-line graphs. The materials were
self-correcting. The children were asked to follow the sequence
from picture graphs through double-line graphs but could choose
randomly from within each subgroup of study guides. They were

allowed to work with the material at their own rate and were encouraged to check with each other or the teacher as the need arose. A test incorporating all four types of graphs was designed for use after all twelve of the study guides had been completed.

Activity Cards

A pack of activity cards can add a dash of spice to drill and practice. It can vary the diet of seatwork and independent study. Yet it is nothing more than a slightly different format for the same kinds of questions and exercises we often ask children to do.

Size is important. About half of an 8½ by 11 inch piece of cover stock or oak tag makes a comfortable size for most children to handle. This size allows room for several questions or exercises, but limits the over-zealous teacher. Somehow, it seems less threatening and more fun to pick up four cards with six math examples each than to be handed a ditto sheet with the same twenty-four examples all set out in rows and columns. Perhaps there is something satisfying in quickly completing a task and being able to physically set it aside and begin another short term task. At least it represents a variation in kinds of materials, and children often do more exercises and do them more willingly with such cards.

The way in which exercises are presented on activity cards is also important and is partly responsible for their popularity. Every effort should be made to create provocative and game type exercises. If you wish to make a set of activity cards which will give practice in addition and subtraction, magic squares with missing numbers will provide the same amount of drill and be lots more fun to do than conventional addition and subtraction examples. Word puzzles, like "one way" cross-word puzzles, are more interesting than "fill in the blanks" and provide the same opportunities to use new vocabulary words or to practice writing spelling words. It is more fun to unscramble and write sentences (with correct capitalization and punctuation) than it is to "copy the following sentences correctly."

The variety of exercises which can be put on activity cards is extensive. The "Stretch Your Thinking" exercise and Vocabulary Classification activity illustrated in Chapter Four are two examples. Science and math problem cards discussed at several points throughout the book illustrate other forms of activity cards. Whenever the exercises on, an activity card require specific answers, these answers may be printed on the back of the card making it a self-correcting activity. For activities which are open-ended in nature or which can have many correct responses, no attempt would be made to list answers on the back. A few suggested responses could be given in some cases if it were clearly understood that these were merely *some* of the possibilities.

Cards to Sort

Instructional games and manipulative devices give additional variety to your instructional materials. They can often be made to permit self-correction. You can design sorting games and activities for use by a single child as well as some for two or more players. For this type of activity the child needs a set of cards to be sorted, some indication of the criteria for sorting them, and an answer key. The cards in the set might have on them any of the following kinds of things.

Pictures	Numbers
Letters	Words
Sentences	Clock faces
Parts of sentences	Illustrations of fractions
Roman numerals	Paragraphs
Parts of comic strips	Consonant blends
Maps	Geometric figures

The children might be asked to match two sets of cards; for example match headlines with newspaper articles, clock faces with times given in numerals, or maps with pictures of mapped regions. Other activities might call for a child to sort the cards according to certain classifications such as equivalent fractions or geometric figures. Sometimes the instructions may ask the children to sort the cards into a series or sequence such as these:

Arrange the pictures into a comic strip story.
Put the Roman numerals in order.
Arrange the words into a sentence.
Arrange the sentences into a paragraph.

Arrange the paragraphs into a story.
Make a time line of these events.

There are, of course, many other ways in which cards could be sorted, but these suggestions will give you a few jumping-off places for designing your own Cards-to-Sort activities.

SUMMARY

A wide range of instructional materials is necessary to provide the flexibility and variety required in a program of differentiated instruction. Commercial materials can often be used to meet some of your needs. Frequently reorganizing these materials makes it possible to create multilevel, self-pacing activities.

You will also find it possible to supplement commercial materials with teacher-made items. Tests, job sheets, and study guides are a few of the ways in which you can supplement textbooks and other commercial materials to make them better serve your purposes. Job sheets may be prepared to guide pupils through a series of related or nonrelated activities. Study guides provide direction, guidance, and feedback for the pupil working on a relatively short term activity.

You will often find it necessary to design original materials for specific purposes and specific children. These may take the form of single exercises, a series of similar activities, or a long term program consisting of a variety of related activities. Activity cards may be designed to contain only a few examples or exercises presented in a gamelike or puzzle form, often self-correcting. Such cards help to make drill and practice more enjoyable. Additional variety and spice can be supplied in the form of sorting activities. These can provide some of the essential concrete or semiconcrete experiences elementary school youngsters need before they are ready for more conventional symbolic work.

When selecting, supplementing, or organizing a set of instructional materials for use by children, it is of vital importance to consider the appropriateness of the material or activity for the group of children who may be using it. The goals and objectives for which a given set of instructional materials is being designed will guide your selection of the format and the content of the activities you structure.

FIFTEEN

Preparing Records and Organizing Materials for Instructional Packages

The preparation of activities for individualizing learning experiences involves considerations beyond the selection or design and production of materials. Arrangements for keeping records and evaluating pupils must be provided. These should be built into the program or series of activities at strategic points. Some records should be kept by pupils, others by teachers. Evaluation should occur throughout a program—perhaps more frequently when self-directing, self-correcting materials are being used.

Attention must also be given to the physical organization of materials and space. You will need to consider various ways of assembling your materials into kits or other instructional packages which can be used directly by the students. Ways of housing and handling these learning packages need to be planned so as to permit ease of maintenance as well as efficiency and effectiveness in use.

This chapter offers suggestions for attending to these aspects of preparing materials for individualized learning activities.

RECORD KEEPING

Keeping track of individual students who are working at different levels and in different materials need not be complicated or unduly time consuming. First, determine what you must know about a pupil who is working in a program and how often you will need this information. You will then be able to design various kinds of simple record sheets for the pupil and/or you to keep. The purpose of each record will dictate its design. Evaluation devices for determining readiness, diagnosing weaknesses, providing feedback on progress, and determining the degree of mastery achieved should be built into every set of instructional materials or activities which requires more than a few days to complete.

Pupil-Kept Records

Record forms to be maintained by the student must be simple enough to enable him to keep them without teacher assistance. Some initial training may be necessary in some cases, but this should be of such a nature that it can be accomplished quickly. Pupil-kept records should require a minimum of a pupil's time. Extensive remarks or complicated mathematical formulas for finding scores should be avoided.

These records must be clear enough to show you at a glance what a child has done and what he is currently doing. In a program where there is a sequence of activities, the child might use a check list and merely check off each one as it is completed. Where activities may be selected in random order, a control sheet could be prepared which identifies each activity by number or title. The child circles the number of the activity he is currently working on and marks an X through the circle when he has finished it.

You will probably also want some quick indication of the kinds of success a child is having with the program. Bar graphs can be kept to show scores in programs where this would be appropriate. On some record forms a simple chart showing "Possible Correct Responses" for each activity could provide a space for the child to fill in "Actual Correct Responses." A subjective rating scale could be provided in some cases. Here the child might be asked to give his own evaluation of his work by checking whether he felt his work on a given activity was Exceptionally Good, Satisfactory or Unsatisfactory.

Often a single record form can be designed to accomplish both purposes—to show progress and to indicate success. An example of such a pupil-kept record is shown in Figure 15-1.

Control Sheet and Progress Graph
Spelling—Level III

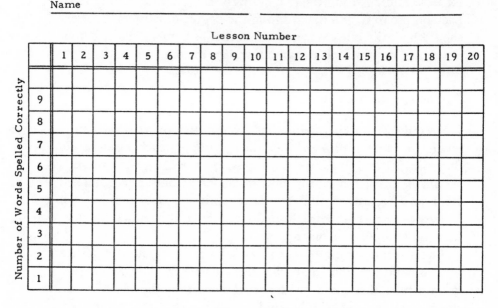

Figure 15—1

This control sheet and progress graph is used with a multilevel spelling program. The child circles the number of the lesson he is currently working on. When he has finished the lesson he fills in the appropriate number of sections on the bar graph to show the number of words spelled correctly on the test. Children work in pairs in this spelling program, giving each other pretests and mastery tests. Each child has his own control sheet and progress graph which he keeps in his spelling folder.

Teacher-Kept Records

In your attempts to provide continuous progress for each child you will find carefully designed records are an absolute necessity. You will use these more to assist you in planning a child's instructional program than to provide a basis for marking a child's performance in terms of grade level expectations. The design of specific record forms will depend upon the purposes for which they will be used. Several kinds of forms will be required to give you the data necessary for your planning.

Individual pupil profiles will assist you in determining instructional levels and in pinpointing specific strengths and weaknesses. Such data is essential in the setting of objectives and in the selection of learning activities for a child. Pupil profile forms can be designed to give you a general overview of a child's academic achievements. Others will provide you with information in greater detail in specific areas such as reading and math. You will also find it valuable to have some record of a child's social and study habit patterns.

Figure 15-2 illustrates one example of a pupil profile for reading which an intermediate teacher designed for his own use. This form can be kept largely by recording scores, although some written data is needed in the section relating to basal readers. Space is provided on the back of the form for teacher comments, statements of objectives, and suggestions for possible activities.

Other records you will need for each pupil include individual progress forms and cumulative records. Individual progress forms should contain data relative to the specific instructional groups, materials and activities which comprise the tangible aspects of a child's rate of progress, scores on feedback and mastery tests, and any teacher comments. Cumulative records, as they are described here, refer to those records you will be sending to the child's next teacher. You will want these to include information which will make it possible for that teacher to provide continuity in the child's progress. Data summarizing the pupil's program while in your class, listing the materials he has used and completed or needs to complete, noting his scores on mastery tests, and giving your estimate of his instructional and independent study levels should appear on these records.

One other kind of record will be valuable to you in making plans for classroom instruction. This is a class profile sheet. You will find it advisable to have some type of class profile sheet in each of the major instructional areas. Such a record might be in the form of a chart based on your class list providing names of

Pupil Profile—Reading

Botel Inventory   Date Given

Phonics				Word Recognition	Word Opposites	
Consonants	Vowels	Syllables	Nonsense Words		Reading	Listening

Basal Readers

Name of Book	Level	Date Completed	End of Book Test	Comments

Diagnostic Reading Test

_____ Form_____ Date Given_____

(Name of test used)

Subtest						
Score						

Subtest						
Score						

Figure 15–2

all the students and places to record pertinent data related to the subject area. This data could be shown as a check list, a graph, a tally, or a series of scores. Records of this type will assist you in identifying and planning for small groups of children who could be brought together for instruction in specific skills or subskills.

EVALUATION

Evaluation of a pupil's progress implies more than averaging a series of marks to obtain a periodic grade. It involves making judgments about the child's readiness (1) for work in a specific skill, (2) for consideration of a given concept, or (3) for participation in a particular experience. Evaluation includes pinpointing the various strengths and weaknesses a child has. These kinds of information enable you to establish realistic goals for the child and to select routes to those goals which will capitalize upon his capabilities and interests.

When a child is engaged in a series of learning activities it is important for you to have periodic objective feedback about his success as he progresses. This type of data assists you in making decisions about the best way for a child to continue. Should he go on as originally planned? Could he skip parts of the series or sequence? Does he need review or extra practice in some part of the program?

Each of the aspects of evaluation is fully as important as determining how much a child has mastered at the end of a given study. Yet, giving end-of-chapter tests or unit exams and averaging scores often serve as a teacher's whole approach to evaluation.

Evaluation as Ongoing Pupil-Teacher Communication

Children should understand the objectives of any learning sequence which they are pursuing. This is especially true when children are encouraged to work independently. You can help children to become more independent by allowing them to participate in the setting of goals and by arranging for them to become involved in evaluation of their own progress.

One intermediate teacher periodically uses a part of the week for individual "target setting" conferences with the students. A mimeographed form is used to keep a record of each child's personalized targets and the steps which have been chosen to work toward these goals. Targets are not always in a skill or content area, but frequently deal with desired attitudes and behaviors. An example of a record of this type of pupil-teacher conference is shown in Figure 15-3.

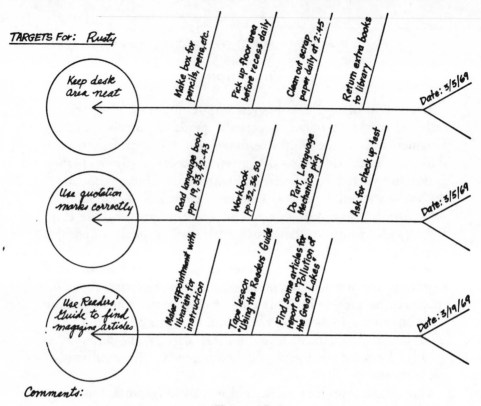

TARGETS For: Rusty

Keep desk area neat
- Make box for pencils, pens, etc.
- Pick up floor area before recess daily
- Clean out scrap paper daily at 2:45
- Return extra books to library

Date: 3/5/69

Use quotation marks correctly
- Read language book pp. 19, 35, 42-43
- Workbook pp. 32, 36, 50
- Do Part, Language Mechanics pkg.
- Ask for check up test

Date: 3/5/69

Use Readers' Guide to find magazine articles
- Make appointment with librarian for instruction
- Tape lesson "Using the Readers' Guide"
- Find some articles for report on "Pollution of the Great Lakes"

Date: 3/19/69

Comments:

Figure 15–3

   These conference records are made in duplicate, one for the student and one for the teacher. The space marked "Comments" may be used by either student or teacher to indicate difficulties encountered, dissatisfaction with pacing or the selection of tasks, special interest or enthusiasm, etc. Teacher and student then confer a second time to evaluate the progress which has been made.

   Another approach to pupil-teacher evaluation has been used by several teachers with good results. The checklist shown in Figure 15-4 was used by these teachers to assist in reporting pupil progress to parents.

   The checklist was also used to involve the students in self-evaluation. Children met with the teacher in small groups to discuss the behaviors on the checklist and to discuss their progress in attaining the desired behaviors. This technique yielded several dividends. The children became more aware of the nature of some of the objectives teachers felt were important for all learners. Talking about their own progress toward these objectives in small group discussions often helped an individual child clarify his own concept of his progress. Children were also able to interpret for their parents the meaning of the marks on the checklist, thereby improving home-school communication.

Dear Parent,

We believe that your child should grow towards responsible independence. We believe that the representative behaviors in the following checklist are characteristic of such growth.

MARKING KEY
1 not yet
2 sometimes
3 usually
4 not yet expected

	Marking Period	
2	3	4

Sets his own goals and objectives and can state what he has been learning
Identifies and builds on own strengths.....................................
Identifies and accepts his own weaknesses................................
Performs to improve weaknesses...
Keeps records of his own progress..
Accepts constructive criticism from others...............................
Expresses his opinions in an acceptable manner and can stand up for
  himself when challenged..
Analyzes his incorrect responses and learns from self-correction.........
Develops some worthwhile idea or project without teacher assignment......
Concentrates on appropriate task to be done at proper time...............
Is willing to attempt..
Seeks new experiences..
Develops his own interests...
Exhibits decision-making skills..
Seeks sources to provide answers to his own questions....................
Seeks the aid of others that he knows are in a position to help him......
Adjusts to change..
Adjusts to classroom routine...
Learns by helping and teaching others....................................
Shares materials and experiences with others.............................
Works independently for periods of   minutes.......................
Defers own wishes if the class would be disturbed by his interruption....
Works on own materials in a way which allows others to work on
  different things at the same time......................................
Respects the property of others as well as his own.......................
Observes school and personal safety rules when not under direct teacher
  supervision...

COMMENTS:

Figure 15-4

PACKAGING, STORING AND USING MATERIALS

You will soon discover that providing a differentiated and varied educational diet for your pupils requires considerable organization and "magic wand" waving. Arranging the physical aspects of the learning environment for efficiency and ease of use is essential. Perhaps the first major problem you will encounter here is that of maintaining order among your instructional materials. When children are responsible for obtaining, using, and returning the items they use and for keeping track of their own projects and work, you may soon have a magnificent mix-up of materials. Careful organization can help alleviate this problem. A second difficulty you may encounter is the lack of space. This is where the magic wand waving (and a little more organization) come in. Even if you are inclined to be a "spontaneous" rather than an "organized" type of person, this is one time when you will find it well worth the time and effort to do some long-range thinking and careful planning about the physical arrangement of your instructional materials and of the classroom space.

Instructional Packages

Study guides, record e ing forms, activity cards, games, and other instructional materials can be packaged in a variety of ways. Loose sheets can be put in clearly labeled thin boxes such as those which originally contained typing paper or ditto masters. They can also be kept in file folders which are then filed in a cardboard container according to activity or subject area. Several exercise sheets, lesson pages, or study guides which are to be used in a series can be stapled together to make a sequential learning package. The answer keys to exercise sheets could be placed at the end of the package or stapled to form a separate package.

When multilevel materials are packaged in file folders, a color coding system can make it easier for youngsters to keep the materials in order. The same color coding can be used to designate the various levels of difficulty of the materials. One teacher uses colors in the order they appear on the color wheel from red to violet. Red signals first-grade level material, orange second-grade level, and so on with violet being used for sixth-grade material. Answer keys are made using appropriately colored ink and labels on file folders repeat the color. The same color coding is used for materials from all subject areas.

Activity cards and cards to sort can be packaged in manila envelopes. Manipulative materials and games are often bulkier, and require the use of cigar boxes, large round candy tins, and shoe boxes for packaging. Crossword puzzles have been pasted inside file folders with the title of the puzzle printed on the front of the folder. A small envelope containing the answer key was pasted just below the printed title. These puzzle folders were placed at interest centers. Jewelry boxes containing cardboard anagrams (made by the teacher) were also provided to be used with the puzzles so that it was not necessary to write on them. One book of crossword puzzles goes a long way when packaged and used in this manner.

Storage Techniques

Boxes of many sizes, shapes, and varieties will be required for the housing and storage of learning packages. Grocery stores, drug stores, and liquor stores are good sources. School supplies are often shipped in boxes which can be put into service in your classroom. Boxes which originally contained tempera paint were used to make "chemistry sets" for several intermediate classes. The dividers which had separated the jars of paint were left in the boxes. Baby food jars and new medicine bottles with droppers were filled with powders and liquids to be used in a series of experiments. One box contained enough "chemicals" for two teams of pupils.

Boxes which are used to house instructional materials should be both attractive and functional. Product names and labels do not add to the appearance or neatness of your room. Most cardboard containers can be covered relatively easily with adhesive backed vinyl, wallpaper, or interior grade wall paint. These should be clearly labeled and the material in them thoughtfully organized so that the children can return completed items to the proper place with minimum effort. If the boxes do not contain too much material they are easier to keep in order and can be moved from place to place by the children. When table and counter space in the classroom is at a premium, these boxes can be stored on shelves or in cupboards and yet be accessible to the children when needed.

You will find a filing cabinet important in helping you organize your own materials. Diagnostic and other evaluative instruments, pupil records, instructional materials not currently being used, ditto masters, transparencies, pictures, and all the "etceteras" a teacher collects need to be instantly available. Many teachers have found that their minimum space requirement is satisfied by a four-drawer filing cabinet. If you do not have metal filing cabinets available, many stationery stores carry corrugated cardboard files and filing boxes which can be used as a substitute.

Bulletin boards can often be brought into service for certain kinds of storage. Manila envelopes containing activity cards, conference forms, pupil record sheets, certain types of games, etc. can be stapled to bulletin boards or hung on pegboard panels. Fixtures can also be used in pegboard to hold packs of cards, several manila envelopes, or stapled packages of lesson sheets as well as shelves for boxes of games and manipulatives.

Routines for Using Materials

Even the most thoughtfully organized and housed material does not maintain itself. The children must accept the responsibility for much of this. There are several things you can do to make it easier for them to maintain the material centers. A few have already been mentioned; house only a few related materials in any one box, label everything clearly, and organize the material into a logical sequence or order.

It is also wise to introduce new materials and activities one at a time. Take plenty of time to train the children in the proper care and use of the materials. As much as possible establish a specific place for each set of materials. You may wish to appoint certain children to check the material centers frequently and to straighten them as needed. Any problems which arise relative to the maintenance of these materials could serve as the basis for some small-group problem-solving discussion activities. The children might bring to your attention some difficulties they are having in using the material and suggest a modification in its organization.

SUMMARY

Record forms to be used with instructional materials should include data regarding both the quantity and the quality of a student's interaction with the materials he is using. Pupil-kept records must be simple enough for children to keep and at the same time quickly reveal needed information to the teacher. Teacher-kept records should provide cumulative in-depth information about each child. Their main purpose is to assist you in the continuous evaluation and planning of his program. Evaluation involves gathering *and using* data about a child's performance. It calls for making judgements and decisions regarding the continuity, direction, and pacing of his instructional program. Every effort should be made to permit the student to be actively involved with setting targets for and evaluating his own progress.

Instructional materials can be packaged in a variety of ways for use in short term or long range activities. The selection, preparation, and organization of housing facilities for instructional packages are important in enhancing their utility and simplifying their maintenance. Provisions also need to be made for establishing routines for the use and upkeep of instructional materials.

Appendix

(Sources of Instructional Materials)

Attribute Games and Problems Series by Elementary Science Study, published by Webster Division, McGraw-Hill Book Company, Manchester, Missouri. Copyright © 1967, 1968, by Education Development Center, Inc.

Bond Clymer Hoyt—Silent Reading Diagnostic Test, published by Lyons and Carnahan, Wilkes-Barre, Pennsylvania.

Botel Inventory, published by Follet Publishing Co., Chicago, Illinois.

Classroom Pictures Series, produced by Fideler Visual Teaching, Grand Rapids, Michigan.

Colorforms, produced by Colorforms, Norwood, New Jersey.

Flexigons, produced by Forde Corporation, Tacoma, Washington.

Language Master, produced by Bell and Howell Co., Chicago, Illinois.

Man in Action, published by Prentice-Hall, Inc., Englewood Cliffs, New Jersey.

Math Workshop, published by Encyclopaedia Britannica Corp., Chicago, Illinois.

News Releases in Chapter Seven, written by Ronald J. Pappert, Floyd Winslow Elementary School, Henrietta, New York.

Password, produced by Milton Bradley Co., Springfield, Mass.

Playtiles, produced by Halson Products, Chicago, Illinois.

PYTHAGORUS® and *SWITCH®* puzzles, produced by Kohner Bros. Inc., East Paterson, New Jersey.

Reading and Thinking Skills, published by The Continental Press, Inc., Elizabethtown, Pennsylvania.

Reading for Understanding, published by Science Research Associates, Inc., Chicago, Illinois.

Rig-A-Jig, produced by Rig-A-Jig Toy Co., Chicago, Illinois.

SCRABBLE, produced by Selchow and Righter Co., Bay Shore, New York.

Wff'n Proof, produced by Wff'n Proof, New Haven, Connecticut.

Teacher-made instructional materials discussed and illustrated in the book were designed and produced by the authors.

Bibliography

(One Dozen Books Which You May Want for Your Personal Library)

Barbe, Walter B., *Personalized Reading Instruction*, published by Prentice-Hall, Inc. An exceptional addition to the library of any teacher who teaches reading. Ways to handle individual pupil conferences and record keeping are explicitly discussed. Mr. Barbe's skills check-lists have proved invaluable to us.

Nuffield Math Project. *I Do and I Understand*, published by John Wiley, & Sons, Inc. Intriguing ways to make math a real and vital learning experience through discovery. Not a teachers' manual or handbook, but an idea book which will stimulate your thinking.

Goodlad, John I. and Robert H. Anderson, *The Non-Graded Elementary School*, published by Harcourt, Brace & World, Inc.

Shaplin, Judson T. and Henry F. Olds, *Team Teaching*, published by Harper & Row.

Dufay, Frank R., *Ungrading the Elementary School*, published by Parker Publishing Company, Inc.

The last three books listed are excellent source books for professional educators who are interested in 'exploring the philosophy and rationale which underlie organizational attempts to individualize instruction.

Cutts and Moseley, *Providing for Individual Differences In the Elementary School*, published by Prentice-Hall, Inc.

National Society for the Study of Education 61st Yearbook, *Individualizing Instruction*.

Goodlad, John I., *School, Curriculum and the Individual*, published by Blaisdell Publishing Company.

The preceding three books have been used by our staff to develop personal commitment to the need to individualize instruction. We also found them excellent as reference books for parents who were interested in what we were trying to do.

Washburn, Carleton W., and Sidney P. Marland, *Winnetka*, published by Prentice-Hall, Inc.

219

Darrow, Helen Fisher, and R. Van Allen, *Independent Activities for Creative Learning*, published by Columbia University Press. The least expensive book in this list, yet filled with teacher-tested ideas—a must for every teacher.

Sanders, Norris M., *Classroom Questions—What Kinds*, published by Harper & Row. A semi-programmed book which can improve a teacher's ability to set valid learning objectives and to construct better evaluation devices.

Raths, Louis E., and Sidney B. Simon, *Values and Teaching*, published by Charles E. Merrill Books, Inc. Working through the sections of this book has changed the lives of many of us and we feel that we understand ourselves and others far better for the experience. Many of the suggested discussion exercises can be used exactly "as is" with very young children.

Index

Index